Unmasking the Covert Female Narcissist

Breaking Free from Manipulation, Gaslighting, and Toxic Relationships

Lucas Taylor

Contents

Introduction   5

1. UNDERSTANDING THE COVERT FEMALE
NARCISSIST   9
What Is a Narcissist?   10
Psychology of Covert Female Narcissism   22
Effects of Narcissistic Abuse   25
Journaling Activity: Is Your Partner a Covert
Narcissist?   29
Key Takeaways   30

2. THE ENSNAREMENT PHASE   32
Warning Signs When Dating a Covert Female
Narcissist   32
How the Narcissist Isolates You From Your
Family, Friends, and Colleagues   40
Protect Yourself Against Narcissists on
Dating Apps   42
Activity: Recognize Narcissists on
Dating Apps   46
Key Takeaways   46

3. THE DISENTANGLEMENT PHASE   49
Ending the Relationship   50
What Happens After the Breakup?   56
Journaling Activity for Narcissistic Abuse
Recovery   63
Key Takeaways   63

4. HEALING AND MOVING ON   66
Healing Stages After Narcissistic Abuse   67
Narcissistic Abuse Therapy   69
Why You Shouldn't Feel Sorry for the
Narcissist   71
Post-Traumatic Growth   73

How to Set Healthy Boundaries in Your Future
Relationships   74
Activities: Boundary-Setting Exercise   78
Key Takeaways   79

5. MOVING FORWARD AND LIVING YOUR
   BEST LIFE   82
Focusing on Personal Growth   83
Building Resilience After a Toxic Relationship   89
Journaling Activity: Create a Personal
Growth Plan   93
Key Takeaways   94

6. HELPING OTHERS AND RAISING
   AWARENESS   96
Sharing Your Story   97
Creating Change   102
What Is the Difference Between NPD and
Having Narcissistic Traits?   103
Activity: Write About Your Experience With
Narcissistic Abuse   105
Key Takeaways   105

7. NARCISSISTIC PARENTING   107
The Narcissistic Mother   108
Coparenting With a Narcissist   117
Activity: Template for Parenting Plan   122
Key Takeaways   122

Conclusion   125
Glossary   130
References   139

Introduction

For a long time, the idea has existed that you only get male narcissists. The focus has been on the stereotypical and aggressive behavior of the stereotypical narcissist.

However, while men are still diagnosed with narcissistic personality disorder (NPD) at higher rates, female narcissists definitely exist and they can be just as abusive as the males. Often, it can be harder to spot them, as they're especially good at shapeshifting and hiding in plain sight. Covert female narcissists are part of this group.

Female covert narcissists can adjust their behavior to be whoever you want them to be. In public, they can be supportive and fun, and others may find it nearly impossible to believe that they change into a toxic and abusive person behind closed doors.

Some female covert narcissists construct a victim persona and they live according to this all their lives. They are the long-suffering wife and mother who has sacrificed everything for their husband and children.

Introduction

Maybe they have a partner or child who suffers from a chronic health condition, which makes it even more difficult for them to keep their family together. They could also be the doormats who are abused at work, doing everything for everyone else, while working long hours and never receiving any gratitude in return.

The female covert narcissist lives an inauthentic life. When you first meet her, she's charming and appears empathetic, but soon, she will be using covert techniques to control you behind the scenes. She can appear to be a wonderful, kind-hearted person, who does charity work and is involved with all the local church activities. She really is the kind of girl you can take home to your parents, and they are very impressed when they first meet her.

As the relationship progresses, she'll leave you wondering what happened to the lovely person you first met, but rest assured, she'll never return to that false persona she used to get you hooked. If you end the relationship, she may use love-bombing techniques to reel you back into the relationship.

The aim of this book is to help you recognize a female covert narcissist and to figure out how to deal with her. Maybe you're in a relationship with someone who you suspect might be a narcissist, but you're not quite sure. Reading this book can help you make up your mind if you should get out of your relationship. It will tell you exactly how to do it, as it's not easy to end things with a narcissist. Even after a relationship has ended, you can still experience challenges with the female covert narcissist, especially if you have children together and you need to coparent.

Introduction

The book also discusses reasons why the narcissist is the way she is, and why it's unrealistic to expect that she will change, even if she tells you she will. Once you can identify her manipulation techniques, you will no longer fall for them.

The repercussions for failing to recognize and deal with a female covert narcissist can be severe. An ongoing relationship with a covert narcissist can take a toll on your emotional and mental health. Your self-esteem will be eroded, and you can develop mental health conditions like depression and anxiety.

A female narcissist will always prioritize her own needs, and since she lacks empathy, she will undermine and devalue you. You can find yourself alone as the narcissist also has the capacity to isolate you from your family and friends by using smear campaigns. Some narcissists are so manipulative that they can make you question your perception of reality, which will also make it increasingly difficult for you to trust your own judgment.

The prolonged exposure to emotional abuse will elevate your stress and anxiety levels, which will weaken your immune system, and you could even develop chronic health problems.

It can be complicated to end a relationship with a female covert narcissist, especially if you also had good times together. You might even prefer to remember the times she was kind to you and try to minimize the abuse by attributing it to stress she was experiencing in her life at that time, or you could even think it is partly your fault that she treated you so badly. Don't become trapped by these thoughts, as it means the narcissist was successful in making you question your reality.

Introduction

Recovering from a relationship with a narcissist can be a long and difficult process. If you struggle with post-traumatic stress disorder (PTSD) symptoms, rest assured that this is normal. You will have to work to rebuild your self-esteem and learn how to set healthy boundaries in your future relationships. It will be to your benefit to seek support from a professional mental healthcare provider. Joining a narcissistic abuse support group can also help you during your recovery.

Ultimately, learning the signs of covert narcissism can help you avoid becoming involved in toxic relationships such as these. It can also help you get out of a relationship with a toxic person and help you set better boundaries for future relationships.

Chapter 1
Understanding the Covert Female Narcissist

You're in a new relationship with a beautiful woman who seems perfect. You go on dates to exciting places and you're sexually compatible. Soon, it seems like you'll be in this relationship for the long term.

Then things start to change. You can't quite put your finger on it at first, but something feels off when you're around your girlfriend. Although the relationship is still positive, you feel emotionally drained after spending time with her. Your family adores her, as she enjoys helping others, and she is involved with charities and the church. Her Facebook profile is full of photos of her assisting the needy, and she tells you this is to make an impression on potential future employers.

You believe everything she tells you until you find out she is having an affair with one of your friends. Amazingly, she manages to turn the scenario around and she becomes the victim in this horrible situation. You didn't give her enough attention, and you worked too much. You were also mean to her on an occasion you can't even remember.

Somehow, you start seeing this woman's side of the story, you forgive her and you carry on in a relationship that becomes increasingly distant and emotionally shallow. She knows how to pull all your strings now, and she uses you as a "handsome boyfriend" prop around her friends.

You feel increasingly disconnected from your family and friends, as you have to spend so much time keeping her happy. You quickly learn to sense her mood changes, and you learn what to do to not get into trouble.

You are left feeling bewildered. If you're struggling to figure out what happened, you've likely crossed paths with a female covert narcissist.

What Is a Narcissist?

The term "narcissist" is used a lot these days, but what does it really mean? Narcissistic people may come across as being selfish and entitled. They seem to think they deserve special treatment and see themselves as gifted and look for praise and recognition.

One thing that all narcissists have in common is a lack of empathy for others. They can fake being empathetic but none are genuinely empathetic.

Even though it doesn't seem like it, narcissists often struggle with self-esteem and anger management issues. The more overt types want to impress people by displaying their wealth, intelligence, beauty, and status.

While there is NPD, it's also possible that someone might only have some narcissistic tendencies.

If narcissistic traits interfere with a person's daily life and affect their ability to have meaningful relationships with others, they can be diagnosed with NPD.

According to the Diagnostic and Statistical Manual of Mental Disorders (DSM) that is published by the American Psychiatric Association, someone must meet 5 of 9 criteria to be diagnosed with NPD (Mitra & Fluyau, 2022).

It's possible to have some narcissistic traits without being a narcissist.

The traits are as follows:

- The person expects to be recognized as superior without having achievements to back them up. They have a grandiose sense of self-importance.
- They believe they should be admired by others.
- The person is preoccupied with fantasies of success, beauty, brilliance, and perfection.
- They believe they're special and should only associate with special people or organizations.
- They believe they're entitled to favorable treatment.
- They exploit others to their own advantage.
- They lack empathy and are unwilling to identify with the needs of others.
- They envy others and believe others envy them.
- Their behavior and attitudes are haughty.

Different Types of Narcissism

There are several main types of narcissism:

- **Overt (Grandiose) narcissist:** Someone with this form of narcissism will display most of the characteristics that are traditionally associated with narcissism, such as an unrealistic sense of superiority and entitlement, and an attempt to dominate others. This type of narcissist also enjoys being the center of attention.
- **Covert (Vulnerable) narcissist:** It can be challenging to spot this type of narcissist as they may appear to be shy, reserved, and even humble. They can be hypersensitive to criticism and also crave recognition and attention from others. They can also be victims who tend to believe they're suffering worse than anyone else around them. They might seem like they want someone to save them but they actually use this as a manipulation tactic.
- **Malignant narcissist:** This type of narcissist can be considered dangerous, as they can be sadistic and aggressive and prey on others. They are malicious and enjoy seeing other people suffer.
- **Somatic narcissist:** This type of narcissist derives their self-worth from their bodies. Some might obsess over their weight and physical appearance. They will usually also criticize others, and take part in toxic behavior like fat-shaming.
- **Intellectual (Cerebral) narcissist:** These people usually regard themselves as more intelligent than everyone around them, and they go out of their way to make others feel unintelligent. You'll ultimately never win an argument with them, so it's best to ignore them.

Covert Female Narcissist

What sets a covert female narcissist apart from other types of narcissists? This type of narcissist is also selfish, wants admiration, and lacks empathy, but is more subtle than an overt narcissist. They tend to use indirect aggression to manipulate others and can engage in passive-aggressive behavior, such as gaslighting and guilt-tripping.

The covert female narcissists may even appear to be emotionally sensitive and humble, but this is just part of their manipulation techniques. They can be charming and often manage to maintain the image of an innocent victim. This makes them especially dangerous, as it's challenging to detect their true nature.

Characteristics

It's not easy to identify a covert female narcissist, but they usually do share certain characteristics.

They tend to suck the energy and happiness out of people, making you feel drained and miserable. It may be difficult to say why. You'll just know that you don't want to be around her and you want to spend as little as possible time with her. She may even come across as a positive and happy person, who accuses others of destroying her good mood. Keep in mind that the female covert narcissist is presenting a fake image to the world and that they don't live authentic lives.

She'll project a false image of who she truly is, which will often be based on the values of the culture and even the family in which she grew up. For example, if she grew up in a wealthy family in which the women were expected to study, find a husband with similar qualifications, get married, and have two children, she might do the same. However, it's likely that she won't really care for her husband and children.

They are simply accessories to her success that can be displayed, as long as she approves of them. If her husband loses his job or money, or he doesn't look after his physical appearance, she will most likely divorce him. In the same way, her children will feel her wrath if they fail at school or sport, gain weight, or just become what she regards as physically unattractive as they grow up.

She will likely expect you to know what she needs without actually telling you. It's challenging to be in a relationship with this type of woman, as she holds you responsible for being attuned to her needs all the time. She can't communicate her emotional needs, and instead, she makes everyone around her feel what she is feeling. The aim of this emotional contagion is to get everyone around her to do everything in their power to make her feel better.

If you fail to meet your covert narcissistic partner's needs, she will almost certainly resort to manipulative techniques such as guilt-tripping and shaming.

The covert narcissist is the eternal victim. Their own suffering is always foremost in their minds, and they don't understand that other people suffer as well and experience difficult times in their lives.

The covert female narcissist can also often be paranoid and believes others are out to get them. They suspect nearly everyone of having ulterior motives and wanting to take advantage of them.

If she does anything wrong, she'll never admit it, even if she's caught in the act. She also has a talent for projecting her bad behavior onto you and making you look like the bad guy in a situation. For example, if you catch her stealing money from your checking account to fund her expensive lifestyle, she'll find a way to become a victim in this scenario.

She'll tell you how much money she'd spend to furnish your apartment, even though you told her not to buy the extravagant and expensive items she insisted on buying. She'll accuse you of being stingy, not appreciating her, and not being willing to invest in your relationship.

A narcissist is unlikely to apologize. If they do say sorry, the apology is usually followed by a "but." For example, "I'm sorry I smashed your laptop, but you made me very angry."

Your narcissistic partner will often have her own version of the truth, and she's a skilled liar. It will be difficult to catch her in a lie as she is adept at fusing lies and half-truths in believable stories. If you manage to catch her in a lie, you need to prepare yourself for gaslighting.

This means she will make you doubt your own memories and perceptions. She could deny that certain things ever happened, tell you that you're remembering things the wrong way, and blame you for things that aren't your fault. A gaslighter might tell you that you're just too sensitive and that you always exaggerate. The only thing you can do in this case is to trust yourself and believe in your memory.

Your narcissist will stubbornly continue to believe in her own truth, even if she is presented with facts that contradict her version of events.

The female narcissist is also good at imitating emotion, even though she is cold, emotionally shallow, and can't really form meaningful connections with others. You might feel distant from your partner, and you can't really talk to her or confide in her.

The reality is she is only interested in a superficial relationship and can't form a strong emotional bond with you. As long as you help her portray the image of a perfect relationship or marriage, she'll be happy with you, otherwise, she'll make sure that you feel her anger.

Covert narcissists are usually incapable of having long-term relationships because they are so needy. They are usually more worried about their own distress than caring for others. When they do form a relationship, they will manipulate their partner. Having a relationship with them is a stressful experience, as you'll end up feeling angry and sad, as well as devalued. It would be in your best interest to speak to a mental healthcare practitioner, who can also help you learn how to set healthy boundaries.

Differences Between Overt and Covert Female Narcissists

While the overt narcissist is arrogant and loves attention, the covert narcissist could be shy and uses passive-aggressive techniques to get what she wants. The covert narcissist is good at hiding in plain sight and uses a false victim persona. Some covert narcissists can even be mistaken for codependents.

Overt Female Narcissist

The overt female narcissist can be charming and bold, and she expects everyone around her to treat her as their superior. She can be highly competitive. A good example are the *Queen Bee* bosses who expect everyone around them in the workplace to submit to them. This behavior is not limited to managers though, and even ordinary overt female narcissistic employees can turn coworkers against each other.

While male narcissists tend to be more aggressive, overt female narcissists tend to be aggressive by being the "mean girl." They are just as dangerous as the males, spreading rumors, gossiping, or using name-calling to hurt people. These are also considered forms of narcissistic abuse.

They can also act out and create a scene, which can even include threatening suicide if they don't get their way.

Covert Female Narcissist

The covert narcissist doesn't loudly broadcast her superiority, but she will tear people down through baiting and gossip.

She can cause chaos in a manipulative way to ensure that she stays the center of attention.

They are usually drawn to people who are caretakers and can satisfy their obsessive need for attention. If they feel that they're not getting enough attention, they might create chaos or some kind of crisis to ensure they get it.

The covert narcissist is also a long-suffering victim who drains the emotional energy from everyone around her. A state of narcissistic collapse is more visible with these types of narcissists.

When a narcissistic injury happens, you'll likely feel as if you need to walk on eggshells around them. The covert female narcissist could get into this state after experiencing some type of disappointment. They will become aggressive and struggle to keep up their false persona. For example, this could happen when they don't get the job offer they wanted, a family member refuses to invest money in their business and whatever else could cause their plans to fail.

Your narcissistic partner may burst into tears, or take her bad mood out on you without an explanation, and you'll just end up being stonewalled.

A covert narcissist is also more likely to suffer from depression and anxiety. They tend to pity themselves and exaggerate their illnesses.

Strategies Used to Influence and Control Their Victims

Not all women with narcissistic tendencies behave in the same ways, but the different types of narcissists use certain strategies to exert control over the people in their lives.

Control Strategies Used by the Covert Female Narcissist

Some well-known techniques used by the covert female narcissist can include the following:

- They can use gaslighting to manipulate you into questioning your perceptions and your memory of events. This technique is especially useful to them if you should confront them about something they did wrong, and they will question how you recollect the events. They could tell you that something didn't happen the way you remember it, and might even tell you that you've got a psychological problem and that you're losing your mind.

- Your covert narcissist may also use the strategy of triangulation. She can bring an outside person into your relationship to create tension and talk negatively about you to this person. She can also use this person's opinion to make you doubt yourself.

- The covert female narcissist may also project her faults onto you. It's a common practice for them to accuse their victims of doing things they're guilty of doing themselves. It also comes down to victim-blaming when they blame the victim in the relationship for all the problems.

- They use silent treatment as a form of punishment to confuse their victims and make them feel anxious. It's also a form of control, as the victim then tries their best to find out what they did wrong and tries to please the narcissist.

- The covert narcissist may also love bomb someone to keep them under their control. This can include giving them lots of attention, affection, and even gifts to gain their trust and love.

- She could also try to use hoovering as a technique to try to control you and win you back if you break up with her. This technique is similar to love bombing, and you could also be showered with gifts and compliments. However, it can also include forms of "stalkerish" behavior, such as sending text messages throughout the day, liking your posts on social media if you're still friends on these platforms or even sending you gifts. If they are successful, you'll be sucked right back into the relationship.

- Another painful technique that the covert narcissist may use against you, is to start a smear campaign where they spread lies among your family, friends, and even coworkers to discredit you. This smear campaign may not be limited to those close to you and she may spread misinformation in wider social circles. You may only become aware of what's going on when you notice people are starting to ignore you or avoid contact. If you say anything about the abuse, you're treated as if you're the one who's causing the problems. If the narcissist loses control over you, they'll try to control how others see you.
- Covert narcissists are especially inclined to start a smear campaign after they have suffered a narcissistic injury. For example, if you've left the relationship and ignored their hoovering attempts.

Control Strategies Used by the Overt Female Narcissist

The overt female narcissist may use some of the following techniques:

- Overt female narcissists can be more intimidating and threatening. They can attempt to use threatening behavior to gain control over you.
- Their behavior is usually more dominant and they can be forceful. They may insist on always being "in charge" in the relationship and wanting to make all the decisions.

- The overt female narcissist can come across as boastful. She tends to exaggerate her achievements to get admiration and can boast about what she has accomplished, to make you feel inferior; for example, if she has a higher-earning job than you and keeps bringing it up in fights. She might tell you that she has the right to make most of the decisions since she earns more than you.
- An overt narcissist may also criticize you at every opportunity she gets to make you feel bad about yourself. This criticism could be focused on your competence and abilities; for example, she could criticize your career choices, or she could make you feel inadequate about your appearance.
- The overt narcissist can also resort to a smear campaign where she will badmouth you to anyone willing to lend her an ear.

Hiding Behind a Codependent Persona

It's possible for a covert female narcissist to hide behind a codependent persona. They may adopt codependent behavior such as caretaking and pleasing others, which may make them appear self-sacrificing, accommodating, and selfless.

Appearing codependent can make it easier for covert narcissists to manipulate others to meet their needs, as they're hiding behind a false persona of helplessness and vulnerability. These types of narcissists are eternal victims that are enabled by those around them who give them sympathy and support. They use this technique to get attention and gain control, without having to act like an overt narcissist.

Not all covert narcissists use a codependent persona, but it can work for them to combine the codependent's desire to please and the covert narcissist's manipulation tactics. It can make it easier for people to trust them. They use the language of codependency to soften their narcissistic tactics, as it is seen as less antagonistic and more helpless. Codependents are often excused for their behavior as they are seen as needy and desperate.

When narcissists appear codependent, it can be to do with their fear of abandonment, need for control, and anxiety, which can also mean that they lean toward vulnerable narcissism.

Vulnerable narcissists are blame-shifters and they usually find something to complain about. Nobody can really do anything right in their eyes.

Despite appearing vulnerable, these types of narcissists possess self-centered tendencies and they need attention, validation, and to be in control in their relationships. They're usually exploitative and manipulative and they struggle to form genuine connections with people due to their tendency to be self-centered and primarily concerned with their own well-being.

Psychology of Covert Female Narcissism

What causes someone to become a covert narcissist? It's important to understand where they learned this behavior and how it impacted them, but remember that it's not your duty to feel sorry for them or save them.

However, gaining a better understanding of their behavior will help your own recovery, as you will understand that their cruel behavior is not about you.

The origin of their narcissism can often be traced back to their families and the childhood trauma they've experienced at the hands of their caregivers, which also means they've never learned any emotional regulation skills.

Narcissists can be described as emotional vampires, who suck the life force and happiness out of other people to feed their own inner emptiness.

The covert narcissist may feel like they have been let down by authority figures, and this has made them obsessed with power and control. They likely experienced trauma in their childhoods which has left them feeling completely powerless and worthless. This is also what is behind their damaging behavior.

It's also speculated that narcissists could be deficient in the area of their brain that is responsible for empathy, as a result of genetics and the result of childhood trauma. (Corelli, 2023)

This predisposes them to callous behavior and also to developing addiction issues. Drug and alcohol abuse will unfortunately make this worse.

This also makes the narcissist incapable of experiencing sophisticated emotions such as love, empathy, or remorse, which they also regard as useless vulnerabilities. The covert female narcissist will attempt to mimic some of these emotions when they love bomb you.

If the covert female narcissist was raised by a narcissistic parent, their true self would have been regarded as unimportant by this parent and would have been discarded. The narcissist may have chosen to become a copy of their abusive parent to survive the environment in which they were raised.

When the narcissist is presented with facts that differ from their "truths," they may experience a microscopic psychotic episode. During this episode, they can become detached from reality and experience episodes of magical thinking and delusions.

They are, unfortunately, doomed to repeat these patterns of abuse that they experienced as children.

Abandonment Fears and Insecurities Among Covert Narcissistic Women

The behavior of some covert narcissistic women can partly be driven by underlying insecurities and fears that they will be abandoned.

Even if they appear confident outwardly, these women may struggle with low self-esteem and they could feel inadequate as a result of past rejection, which could have given them deep-seated fears that they aren't good enough and can never please others.

This could also cause them to look for approval from others to feel better about themselves. Covert narcissists often also fear being rejected based on their appearance, and they could put in a lot of effort to maintain a certain image or look.

Some narcissistic women could be highly driven to succeed in their careers or personal lives as this can also be a way to prove their worth to themselves.

It's vital to remember that whatever fears these women have, it's not an excuse for their reprehensible behavior.

Effects of Narcissistic Abuse

The effects of narcissistic abuse can differ from person to person.

However, the impact of this type of abuse can be severe and long term. It's extremely traumatic, as you've been violated and manipulated, and you've realized that you don't know anything about the person you potentially wanted to spend your life with.

You've experienced psychological violence at the hands of someone who has no empathy. This can cause long-term psychological scarring.

Dissociation is a way of coping with traumatic experiences. You put distance between yourself and the memory of the traumatic event you experienced to protect yourself from pain. This could cause you to become emotionally numb. Some people turn to addictions and obsessions as a way to get away from the horrific reality of what they experienced. The brain blocks the full impact of the horrific experience.

You may also find yourself avoiding anything that reminds you of the trauma—this could be places, people, or anything that may feel threatening to you. You could find yourself acting carefully around people who remind you of the abuser, be it a coworker, manager, or family member, as you don't want to make them angry and then have to go through the same abusive experience again.

If you're still living with the abuser, you're probably acting very carefully, or walking on eggshells around them, to avoid more abuse. You're doing your best to avoid confrontations but still end up being the target when the narcissist is looking for an outlet.

Sadly, you've probably given up on all your needs and desires, to satisfy the needs of the narcissist. Your dreams and goals get pushed onto the backburner as the main aim of your life is to satisfy the needs of your narcissistic partner. She might even be keeping you away from your friends and family, as she wants your life to revolve around her. You need to realize that she'll never be satisfied with what you do for her, even if you give up your entire life for her.

Since becoming involved in a relationship with the female narcissist, you've probably started struggling with health issues you've never experienced before. Chronic stress means your cortisol levels would have shot up, and your immune system may have been compromised which makes you vulnerable to disease. You could also have gained or lost a lot of weight.

You may isolate yourself and struggle to trust others. Many victims of narcissists become hypervigilant after the abuse they suffered at the hands of the narcissist. You could also feel no one will believe you when you tell them what you went through and you possibly feel ashamed. People also tend to blame themselves for the abuse. Even though a therapist may tell you that the abuse isn't your fault, you could still have the fear at the back of your mind that you're somehow not good enough.

It can be tempting to minimize the abuse. You might tell yourself that the abuse isn't that bad, others have suffered worse, or that you've done something to deserve it, or that you provoked her in some way. This is often a survival mechanism that is used in an abusive relationship and could lead to trauma bonds being formed.

A trauma bond happens when you have an intense emotional attachment to your abuser, and it's difficult to break it. This type of bonding often happens as part of a cycle of abuse. The abuser alternates between kindness and cruelty. You may have concocted a belief that these glimpses of kindness are really the narcissist's true character. You tell yourself that her abusive behavior is just the result of stress and that she can't always help her behavior. Some people might even become addicted to the intense emotional experience of trauma bonding.

Trauma bonding makes it even more difficult to leave an abusive relationship—even though they realize it's bad for their long-term well-being. They might be ashamed and could also become dependent on their abuser.

Experiencing suicidal thoughts and thinking about self-harm is a red light and a warning that you should get out of the relationship with the female narcissist as soon as possible. Maybe your circumstances have started to feel unbearable, and you don't think you can continue for another day. In this situation, it's best that you seek help from a qualified mental healthcare practitioner.

Unmasking the Narcissist: Mike's Story

Mike had been dating a woman called Sophia for the last year. She was intelligent and beautiful and had a successful career. He was deeply in love with her, but lately, he had been noticing behavior that has been bothering him.

Soon after this unsettling behavior, she would often turn around and then shower him with attention, affection, and praise. She also usually wanted to be the center of attention and succeeded in turning most of their conversations back to herself.

He had tried to talk to her about some of his concerns, but she just told him he was too sensitive or was overreacting. He thought that this was true when he heard her telling one of her friends that she was lucky to have a boyfriend like him.

Then one day, he invited her to his apartment for a special dinner, as he wanted to ask Sophia to marry him. However, while he was preparing food in the kitchen, he overheard her speaking on the phone to one of her friends.

He was devastated when he heard her tell her friend that she believed she could do so much better than him, as she actually found him boring. However, she also said she had decided to settle for him, as he was a "good catch" with money and a stable career. She also felt she was getting older and she was running out of time to find somebody else.

Mike confronted Sophia, and she tried to deny it at first, but then eventually admitted that she had said those things.

She said that he was insecure and that she didn't mean those things, but Mike saw through her excuses and finally realized that he had been a victim of manipulation for a long time.

Mike decided to end the relationship. Even though it was painful, he decided he deserved better than being with someone who couldn't really love him for who he was.

Journaling Activity: Is Your Partner a Covert Narcissist?

It's not always that easy to determine if you're in a relationship with a covert female narcissist. Writing down a few key ideas could help you:

- Create two columns on a piece of paper, one for negative traits and one for positive traits.
- Write down what you admire about your partner in the positive traits column. These could be any positive qualities like intelligence or a good sense of humor.
- Write down the negative behavior you've noticed in the "Negative Traits" column. This could include manipulative or controlling behavior.
- After you've done this, consider how the traits are spread across the columns. Does she have more positive than negative traits? Do they balance each other out?
- Consider red flags or warnings that you may have noticed. This could include that she always wants to be the center of attention.
- Other warning signs could be if your partner doesn't take responsibility for her actions or if she blames others for her actions.
- If you're still unsure, but you have some concerns about your relationship, it's best to speak to a qualified therapist.

Key Takeaways

- Narcissistic people may act in selfish and entitled ways.
- NPD is a mental health condition.
- Narcissists struggle to have meaningful relationships with others.
- There are different types of narcissism.
- The covert (vulnerable) narcissist is shy and reserved. They may have a victim mentality and want someone to save them.
- The covert female narcissist tends to use indirect aggression to manipulate others. They can engage in passive-aggressive behavior, such as gaslighting and guilt-tripping. Their behavior can be more subtle than that of other types of narcissists.
- It's often difficult to identify the covert female narcissist, as they can also be charming.
- The covert female narcissist projects a false image to the world and doesn't live an authentic life.
- She will often expect you to know what she wants, without her having to tell you. She wants you to be attuned to her needs at all times.
- If you can't meet the female covert narcissist's needs, she may use manipulative techniques such as guilt-tripping and shaming to get her way.
- The covert narcissist rarely admits to doing anything wrong and will project her bad behavior onto others. She is also a good liar.
- The covert narcissist is only interested in forming a superficial relationship and can't form a strong and meaningful bond with you.

- The covert narcissist can use gaslighting to manipulate you into questioning how you remember events and perceive things.
- The covert narcissist will project her faults on you. She will accuse you of doing things she is guilty of doing herself.
- The female covert narcissist can love bomb her victims to keep them under her control at first. This means giving them attention, affection, and even gifts to earn their trust.
- The origin of narcissism can often be traced back to childhood trauma.
- It's important to understand a narcissist's behavior, as this will help you realize that you're not responsible for the way they behave, and it will help your recovery process.
- Some covert narcissistic women have underlying insecurities and fears that they will be abandoned by their partners.
- A relationship with a narcissist can cause psychological scarring.
- A trauma bond is an intense emotional attachment to an abuser that is difficult to break.

Chapter 2
The Ensnarement Phase

Have you been dating a "nice" girl who has suddenly turned into a manipulative and abusive person? Are you struggling to understand what happened? This is because female covert narcissists usually conceal their authentic selves until they have completely trapped you. They first want to win your trust and limit your chances of getting away from them before it's too late.

There might be certain warning signs while you're dating, which will hopefully help you realize that it's in your best interest to look elsewhere for a relationship. Setting strong boundaries will also make you less attractive to narcissists.

Warning Signs When Dating a Covert Female Narcissist

Maybe you're getting a strange feeling about your love interest, but how do you figure out if they're a narcissist? It's not easy, but there are certain telltale signs you can look out for when dating.

One thing about narcissists is that they're usually strange people, and not in a good way. Those who don't know them well may think they're only eccentric, but you, unfortunately, know better.

Even though narcissists are prone to strange behavior, they are also charming and seductive, and you may decide to ignore some fairly obvious red flags.

Push-Pull Behavior

Narcissists can engage in push-pull behavior, which can be confusing. They could show a lot of interest in you, and then suddenly withdraw.

In the "push" phase, they will give you a lot of attention and affection. They could give you compliments and affection and make you feel desired.

During the pull phase, the narcissist could withdraw and start to act indifferent toward you. They could ignore your phone calls, not respond to your messages, and cancel plans.

Their behavior can leave you feeling confused and insecure about your relationship. This type of behavior is already a form of control the narcissist is trying to use over you. They want to swing the power balance in their favor by keeping you off-balance and uncertain about their real intentions.

Just keep in mind that not everyone who displays this type of behavior is a narcissist, and unresolved trauma or anxiety could also be part of the reason why your partner is pulling away from you. If you experience this type of behavior with your partner, you need to communicate openly with them about your feelings and look for help, if you need it, or if you strongly suspect your partner could be a narcissist, it may be in your best interest to end the relationship.

A Lack of Boundaries

The narcissist won't respect your boundaries. They feel they're entitled to your time and attention, and they don't see how their behavior violates your boundaries. They feel that social norms and rules don't apply to them, and they don't respect the autonomy of others.

So, how do you deal with a narcissist who doesn't respect your boundaries? You'll often find the people in your life who get upset when you set boundaries, to protect your time and space, are those who benefitted when you didn't have any.

Setting Boundaries

Setting boundaries when you're dating has the positive side-effect of making you less attractive to narcissists. When you're not constantly available to give them attention and boost their self-esteem, they'll try to find what they need elsewhere.

Narcissists always need to be in control, and boundaries are obstacles in their path. They might also see boundaries as questioning if they're right, and according to them, they're always right. They will become angry when it means your boundaries mean they have less access to you. This attitude may cause them to ignore your boundaries.

The narcissist you're dating may see your boundaries as a personal attack and push back against them. For example, if you don't want to be contacted after 8 p.m. when you're home, they might still insist on sending you messages or phoning you at all hours of the day and night. She expects you to be available any time she needs attention or support.

She could react in various dysfunctional ways when you establish boundaries. She could say anything to belittle your decision and could even accuse you of being oversensitive.

She might make a manipulative game out of it by totally ignoring your boundaries, and looking for weaknesses that will help her get past your boundaries.

You can expect emotional abuse and the narcissist will become defensive. When they become defensive, they'll show you how entitled they really are and that they're just bothered by the fact that they can't act how they want to. This will give you a clear indication of how little they actually care about you.

Unfortunately, setting boundaries also lets the narcissist know what is important to you, and can give them ammunition to use when they want to hurt you. It's a risk worth taking to avoid becoming one of their pawns who live to satisfy their needs and whims.

If you feel that setting boundaries has just made your narcissistic partner angry, or that it has given them more ammunition to use against you in the relationship, what can you really do about it? This type of behavior is a warning sign that it might be in your best interest to leave the relationship as early as possible.

When you're in a relationship with the narcissist and things aren't going well, the one thing you have to accept is that she can't change. You won't be able to bring back her fake persona that you first met and fell in love with.

The best thing you can do for yourself is to set boundaries and let her go.

Mood Swings and Narcissistic Rage

You may notice that your narcissistic partner is prone to mood swings and even rage. Their behavior often seems like an overreaction to small disappointments or mistakes, that can even cause them to explode in a rage. It will feel as if they've undergone a personality change in a split second.

If anything has ruined their mood, they will be angry for an extended period, and they see everything that happens around them as bad. Every day, small things that go wrong, for example, if the waitress forgets to bring them a fork, can lead to an angry outburst. They'll be angrier every time something else "goes wrong."

They act hostile to everyone around them, even though that person had nothing to do with whatever it is that made them angry in the first place.

Their mood could lift if something good happens, for example, her father sends her money to pay off some of her accounts. However, when something else goes wrong, she'll revert to her bad mood.

The narcissistic rage is partly caused by the narcissist's fear that people will find out she's not the person she says she is. The narcissist is thin-skinned, and anything or anyone that challenges her perceived superiority can set off her rage.

What makes narcissistic rage different from other types of anger is that it's completely out of proportion to what provoked it and usually takes people by surprise.

Outward signs of narcissistic rage can include an explosive outburst of screaming and yelling that the narcissist seems unable to control. It's usually a fit of anger and the narcissist can also become verbally or physically aggressive.

Inward signs can be when she gives you the silent treatment, behaves in a passive-aggressive way, and doesn't do things she is supposed to do. She can also become sarcastic and appears to be hostile and bitter.

Narcissistic rage is a childish way of acting, as the person can go from being annoyed to a full-blown outburst in a matter of minutes.

The reasons for this terrible display of rage are usually also quite childish and often won't make sense to you. It often has to do with the narcissist's self-esteem being threatened. She could lash out in a rage because she didn't get her way, or she didn't get enough attention and felt ignored. She might also lash out in a rage if she feels she's losing control of people or a situation.

Rumination and Grudges

You'll also notice that the narcissist can't let go of a grudge and can keep on thinking about an event or situation over and over again. This puts them in a bad mood and they can become irritable, depressed, and anxious.

The focus is usually on their own feelings and how they've been hurt or slighted. They will ruminate about why they're not receiving the validation they believe they should receive.

Intermittent Reinforcement

Another reason why it's difficult to leave a relationship with a narcissist is that it isn't always bad. In fact, she may actually treat you pretty well on some days. Narcissists use intermittent reinforcement to control the people around them. They assume giving you praise and attention at times will keep you interested in the relationship, while it also allows them to keep their power over you.

When she abruptly withdraws her approval, you'll become confused, and if you really want her in your life, you may feel that you need to work harder.

The narcissist will also withdraw if she wants to punish you if you've offended her in some way.

Covert Female Narcissist's Persona

The narcissist will often portray herself as the ideal partner and companion. However, what you see is usually not what you get.

Covert narcissists usually have many codependent traits and they're usually disconnected from their true selves.

The goal of the covert narcissist is to preserve the persona she has created for herself. They usually have to be either the victim or hero in the story, and sometimes even both.

You need to understand that she believes in this false self and that she's not consciously playing a role.

The following are often characteristics of the covert narcissist's false persona:

- She's too nice, so she gets abused by other people.
- She's not that smart and needs help when it comes to doing certain things. She can't do certain things for herself, and that's why she gets manipulated.
- She's too passive to stand up for herself.
- She's too generous and everyone's doormat.
- She always puts others first and wants everyone to be happy, even if it's at her expense.
- She had a traumatic childhood and managed to turn her life around.
- She worked hard for certain things; for example, for her career or her family, but things were taken away from her.

The covert narcissist who believes this narrative will live her life in a way that makes it true. She will get a lot of narcissistic supply from her flying monkeys. These are people she will surround herself with who enable and validate her behavior, and from whom she can get a consistent stream of attention, praise, compliments, and flattery.

The narcissist will tell her flying monkeys her story of being victimized, as they know the confidants will spread the story, and will also affirm that they deserve more. The flying monkeys will also constantly check up on them and offer them support. This victim persona gets them the attention they crave.

It's not possible to give a narcissist with this type of persona what she wants, as she gets more narcissistic supply when she complains about how bad her life is. Therefore, if she gets what she wants, she won't have any narcissistic supply.

The covert narcissist will look for opportunities to create the narrative that they were victims who couldn't set boundaries, and who were "forced" into doing something they didn't really want to do. For example, she might encourage you to buy a new car and act excited about it, but then she spends years telling everyone she doesn't want that car and that it's actually a huge waste of money.

How the Narcissist Isolates You From Your Family, Friends, and Colleagues

When you're in a relationship with a narcissist, she will isolate you from your family and friends because she doesn't want you to have a support system in place. This makes it easier for her to control you.

Isolation is one of the most popular forms of abuse used by narcissists.

The narcissist will not only isolate you from everyone around you but also your own values, beliefs, and sense of reality. Most people also don't really understand NPD, which causes people who are abused by narcissists to be isolated even further.

The narcissist will isolate you from yourself, by using cognitive dissonance (a conflict between what you perceive as the truth and what they tell you is happening). They will deny your reality and they will cause you to start doubting yourself.

Narcissists often isolate their loved ones from the outside world, as they're afraid they will be revealed as false, and not as the superior beings they make themselves out to be. Narcissists are usually careful about what information about themselves is exposed to others. They'll make it clear to you that you can't speak about certain things and that you shouldn't speak about problems in your relationship to anyone else.

Narcissists also tend to isolate their family members by turning them against each other. They create a threatening atmosphere through rage and blame and usually isolate their partners by belittling and threatening them and through violent outbursts.

The narcissist will keep you away from your friends, especially if they're female, and you may be accused of having lovers. You also won't be able to make new friends, as catering to the narcissist's needs will take up most of your time.

Very few people can actually imagine narcissistic abuse unless they lived with it themselves. They might even dismiss the experience of survivors, which can isolate them further. It's a complex and destructive experience that causes lasting harm to people.

In the end, they'll isolate you from anything important to you. Many people even find themselves giving up on their hobbies and passions in their life to please their narcissistic partner.

You may try to hang on to what is important to you and what gives you joy, but in the end, it might not seem worth it to listen to hours of the narcissist's nagging. However, these things shape your identity and sense of self. When you lose them, you'll eventually lose your authentic self.

Some narcissists will even sabotage your career or studies. They might accuse you of working too hard and not spending enough time with them. You could end up losing out on the promotion at work you've wanted for a long time, and they'll then accuse you of not being ambitious enough and not being able to give them what they deserve.

Protect Yourself Against Narcissists on Dating Apps

It's becoming increasingly popular to meet your romantic partners online. You can use a dating app like Tinder to create a profile and then browse other users' profiles and communicate with them by sending messages, video calls, or whatever available means you prefer.

It's become a convenient way to meet potential romantic partners who may share your interests and goals. However, online dating sites are also a hunting ground for narcissists.

It's easy for narcissists to present themselves as being flawless online. They simply create a dating profile that highlights their best qualities and doesn't mention their vulnerabilities and flaws. They present an attractive false image to potential partners who can be attracted by their perceived confidence.

The problem with online dating platforms is that they provide predators such as narcissists access to multiple victims, and they're often not held accountable for their deeds.

Some narcissists have also become experts at manipulating the online dating system. They can manipulate the system in their favor in different ways, for example, they could create fake profiles to boost their visibility and they can create fake reviews or ratings to make themselves more desirable to potential partners.

Dating apps and websites also make it easier for narcissists to use their charm to target vulnerable individuals. Covert narcissists have a talent for spotting people who are insecure and lonely.

How to Avoid Becoming a Victim

It's possible to avoid becoming entangled with narcissists on the internet.

It might be a good idea to take a break from online dating and spend some time with people in the real world. Try to meet some new people based on your hobbies and interests. Communicate with people in more authentic ways, such as having face-to-face conversations.

It's entirely possible to meet good people online, but narcissistic predators use these online sites to hunt down their next victim. The problem with these websites and apps is that they allow these shapeshifters to change their identities to make themselves more attractive to their future victims. Some of these dating sites can also link to social media sites, which makes it even easier for emotional predators to create a fake persona that appeals to their potential victims.

Another tip is to take it slow when you participate in online dating. A red flag is when someone wants you to share intimate information too soon or wants to share this type of information with you. Don't share too much information about your career, income, or previous relationships too soon. Get to know someone slowly, so that you can end things before they go too far, if you start to become uncomfortable.

Be careful if someone seems to share all your interests and likes all your favorite places. They may just be love bombing you to trap you in a relationship.

If you want a long-term relationship via a dating app, you'll have to stick to your standards. For example, don't give in to demands for casual sex. You're less likely to meet a narcissist if you have high expectations of a relationship and of being treated with respect.

It's sometimes possible to recognize a narcissist from their dating profile. If they sound too amazing, they probably are. They will have beautiful photos on their profile that have probably been arranged to make them seem like they are fun, sophisticated, wealthy, and successful people.

If you do become involved with a covert female narcissist, you're in danger of emotional abuse and of becoming isolated from everyone and everything important to you. Many covert female narcissists also use their partners for financial gain. They expect financial support, or they want expensive gifts. They could even try to control their partner's finances.

It's vital to set boundaries to avoid becoming a victim of the covert female narcissist's manipulative behavior. You need to educate yourself about manipulative behavior and prioritize your well-being above the expectations of a manipulative partner.

The Professional Victim: Stella's Story

In her own eyes, Stella was a helpless victim who always needed to be rescued, or others to help her. She had become adept at manipulating others to feel sorry for her and take care of her needs.

She had been in multiple relationships, and always blamed their failure on her partners' shortcomings. She was always a victim when things went wrong and could never take responsibility for her mistakes and failures.

Her family was also fed up with her need for attention and her victim mentality, but this didn't register with Stella.

She decided to try online dating to find someone who would help her make her life less lonely. She created a profile that presented her as a kind person who has had to deal with a lot in life, and she soon received messages from a lot of men.

However, Stella soon realized she wasn't attracting potential rescuers, but men who were trying to take advantage of a woman they saw as vulnerable. However, she manipulated the men to get gifts and favors.

She eventually became very skilled at manipulating her online suitors, but she never returned their affection or showed interest in them as people.

Stella was eventually exposed and was called out on her manipulative behavior by one of her potential suitors.

Despite this setback, Stella refused to change, as she believed other people owed her attention and admiration. Her relationships suffered more, but she would always find ways to justify her behavior and blamed others for her problems.

She became more isolated as she got older, as she had destroyed so many relationships in the past.

Activity: Recognize Narcissists on Dating Apps

A few simple steps can help you identify narcissists on a dating app:

- Before you even attempt online dating, make sure you know what the characteristics of narcissists are. Learn what you can about all types of narcissists and armor yourself with as much information as possible. It can only help you on your journey.
- Create a list of certain red flags you should look out for, when you scroll through dating profiles. Excessive self-promotion should be easy to spot, but a need for constant attention and a lack of empathy won't be so easy to see. Also look out for people who excessively seem to present themselves as do-gooders; for example, there are many photos of their charity work, and so on, online.
- Watch out for women who have "I don't do drama" on their profiles. Often, these are the women who constantly create it. This is another way to lure people, as most normal people don't want drama in their lives.
- Once you've selected people who you potentially want to contact, ask a friend or family member to give input as well. They might be able to pick up the red flags you've missed.

Key Takeaways

- You can usually recognize covert narcissists by certain behavioral characteristics.

- Narcissists are prone to strange behavior, but they can also be charismatic and charming.
- Narcissists use push-pull behavior by showing attention to you and then withdrawing.
- The covert female narcissist won't respect your boundaries, as she feels entitled to your time.
- Setting boundaries when dating will make you less attractive to narcissists, as it threatens their need to be in control.
- The narcissist will look for weaknesses in your boundaries and try to find ways to get past them.
- When you're dating a narcissist, you'll have to accept that you initially fell in love with a fake persona.
- Narcissists are prone to mood swings and narcissistic rage. They can become irrationally angry about small things.
- Narcissistic rage can present as explosive outbursts.
- Narcissists can't let go of grudges and tend to ruminate about them. They focus on their own feelings and how they've been hurt by the other person.
- It can be difficult to let go of a relationship with a narcissist as she won't treat you badly all the time, and things can be very good on some days.
- Covert female narcissists often build themselves a victim persona and live accordingly.
- The covert female narcissist believes in the persona she creates, and she isn't consciously playing a role.
- The narcissist won't only isolate you from everyone around you, but also from your true self.
- If you don't have a support system in place, it's easier for her to control you.

- Abuse survivors are further isolated by the fact that very few people actually understand narcissistic abuse.
- If you do online dating, it's important to be wary of narcissists.

Online dating makes it easy for narcissists to present fake images of themselves to potential targets.

Chapter 3
The Disentanglement Phase

It can be complicated to end a relationship with a covert female narcissist. One of the first and most important steps you need to take is realizing the relationship has to end as it will only bring you more grief and heartache in the long run.

Ending a relationship with a narcissist is easier said than done, and you need to prepare yourself that there will be challenges involved. Your ex will likely try to manipulate you into coming back into the relationship. Or, if she doesn't get her way, she may try to get revenge in all kinds of nasty ways such as starting a smear campaign against you.

If you have children with your narcissist a breakup can be especially challenging. It means you won't be able to go no-contact, and you need to maintain a civil relationship for the sake of the children. However, you need to stand firm in your decision to end the relationship, set healthy relationship boundaries and look after your own mental health.

Ending the Relationship

Realizing that your relationship with a covert female narcissist is toxic and needs to end is a vital step in your healing process. It is important for the following reasons:

- You will often feel confused and even traumatized in your relationship with a female narcissist. Your partner likely lacks empathy and has manipulated and exploited you. The time you've had with her could have caused you significant emotional damage.
- A relationship with a narcissist is one-sided, with one party putting in all the work. Narcissists only care about their own desires, and they don't care about what you feel or think, as long as you satisfy their needs. This could leave you feeling undervalued and unloved.
- Your narcissistic partner can control and manipulate you to the extent that you lose your own identity. You can become unsure of yourself and develop low self-esteem.
- A relationship with a toxic person will have a negative impact on anyone's mental health, and you could develop mental health issues such as depression and anxiety. You could even develop PTSD.
- At some point, you're going to have to realize the relationship is never going to improve. Narcissists are incapable of change and they will only manipulate you to stay in the relationship. Realizing that this relationship is damaging to your

psychological well-being is a step toward setting boundaries, reclaiming your life, and moving on.

Challenges of Ending the Relationship

The narcissist will probably tell you the end of the relationship is all your fault. You will be the "bad guy,"—the one who threw away the best thing he had in his life. Many narcissists can't let go, and they'll try to convince you that you've made a mistake and that you should take them back.

They'll try to be persuasive and will provide you with reasons why you shouldn't leave the relationship. They'll tell you that you're overreacting, or that you've just misinterpreted their behavior as nasty, that they've just been acting out as they've been under a lot of stress, and that you shouldn't be taking their behavior personally.

If you analyze their behavior, you'll realize that their reasons are actually veiled criticisms of what you're doing and they're just trying to manipulate you into not leaving.

They may also tell you that you're nothing without them and that you'll regret leaving them when they find someone else, or you will be jealous if they are successful in some way.

Your partner may try to guilt-trip you into staying and will want to pull you back into the relationship by reminding you of the good times you had together or the nice things they've done for you in the past. If that doesn't work, they can start blaming, name-calling, and even displaying passive-aggressive behavior.

The narcissist may change tack if she sees her other behavior isn't working to pull you back in. She might suddenly be sorry that she's hurt you in any way and promise to go for therapy. She'll do anything you want or do things the way you want her to do them. You may get fresh hope and think the narcissist finally understands you. However, this won't last long. If you rekindle the relationship, the narcissist will soon revert to her arrogant and inconsiderate behavior. If you've given her another chance, you'll eventually learn that you can't trust this behavior.

When you leave the narcissist, you should try to cut contact as much as possible. However, the narcissist will try to get your attention in all kinds of dysfunctional ways, for example, by sending you messages or phoning you at all hours of the day and night. Unfortunately, this will add a lot of stress to the situation.

Your former partner may also attempt to start smear campaigns against you, such as on social media. She may try to get your friends on her side. She'll try to get sympathy by making you out to be the bad guy.

Some female narcissists may also resort to stalking behavior. They may suddenly appear at an event you're attending, or you see them walking past your house. They want to remind you that they're still around.

If you have decided to break up with your narcissistic partner, it's best to be as prepared as you can possibly be. Write everything down that you're planning on doing and saying.

Make a list of the precise reasons you're leaving the person. This will help you hold on and believe in your reality if the narcissist tries to distort it. Reading the list will help keep you grounded and you'll be able to see through the narcissist's motives.

Make sure that you block all avenues by which your narcissistic ex can contact you. Remove them from social media and block their phone number. Set clear boundaries and don't give them a chance to manipulate you. If they can't contact you, they can't guilt-trip you into coming back to the relationship.

Narcissistic Hoovering

Some narcissists may want to stay "friends" with you for selfish reasons. This type of behavior is called hoovering because the aim is to suck you back into a relationship.

The female covert narcissist is an expert at manipulation and knows how to appeal to you on an emotional level. They could make romantic gestures or appeal to you for help. They could try to seduce you by pretending to be empathetic, love bombing you or even telling you that they're willing to reform. They could arrange physical encounters where they bump into you or employ your friends and family as "flying monkeys" to do their bidding.

The most common types of hoovering are the following:

- **Love bombing:** Your ex will overwhelm you with love and attention to try to drag you back into the relationship. She will try to communicate with you constantly and could even give you gifts.
- **Pity playing:** She might try to get emotional support or sympathy from you by portraying herself as a victim of her problems. For example, she could tell you she couldn't help her behavior toward you, as she has mental health problems. She also wants you to feel guilty about leaving her.

- **Guilt-tripping:** They blame you and want to make you feel guilty for ending the relationship. They could tell you they've sacrificed a lot for the relationship and that you're making them feel bad.
- **Future faking:** The narcissist is trying to draw you back in by promising that she will change. She plans to go for therapy and she commits to changing her behavior. She even wants to make plans with you. However, all these promises usually don't last long, and as soon as she's drawn you back in, she will revert to her old behavior.

When it comes to hoovering, you have to stay strong and avoid being sucked back into the toxic relationship, which will just cause more emotional damage in the long run.

Why Narcissists Hoover

If you want to understand why narcissists hoover, you need to accept that they don't see relationships in the same way you do. They don't have empathy and can't see you as a separate human being from themselves. They don't want a relationship for the sake of love, but they want access to resources such as money, sex, or status. They're basically looking out for their own interests.

Narcissists need a narcissistic supply. This is the attention and admiration that they need from others to be able to maintain their inflated sense of self-worth. They usually need constant praise and admiration to boost their fragile egos and self-esteem.

The narcissist's supply can come in different forms such as praise, admiration, and attention. However, some also thrive on fear and envy from others. They may feel empty and worthless without a constant stream of supply.

They struggle to deal with rejection, and if they weren't the ones who decided to end the relationship, they'll see it as a massive humiliation, due to their underlying insecurities. They might even try to restart the relationship and then break up with you after a while, to get back the power they feel they've lost.

If you're forced to deal with a hoovering narcissistic former partner, the best way to deal with the situation is to try to ignore the behavior. Go no-contact if possible, as this can also help you recover from the breakup faster. Also, don't look at photos of your ex or visit their social media account.

Going "Grey Rock"

If you still have to communicate with the narcissist, the safest option is to use the "grey rock" strategy.

Going grey rock means to "make yourself as uninteresting or unresponsive as possible" when you communicate with the narcissist. Don't give them reasons to be romantically interested in you. Only provide them with essential information when you communicate with them. Minimize emotional reactions and be as nonengaging and uninteresting as possible.

The grey rock strategy refers to being as boring and uninteresting as a grey rock. This behavior works well with a narcissist who is looking for attention from someone. The aim is to create distance from the narcissist without provoking a negative reaction. This type of behavior can reduce the power the narcissist has over you.

What Happens After the Breakup?

Unfortunately, it's not easy to break up with a narcissist and you're probably also going to have to deal with the fallout. Always remember that the narcissist can't be regarded as a fully developed adult person. They often react in childish ways to situations.

When it comes to breakups, it's also more likely that the narcissist will break up with you than that you will break up with them. Psychologists have found that many narcissists can only sustain a relationship for a few months up to a few years. However, sometimes, they will try to hoover you back into the relationship.

When the narcissist is really finished with you—their prey—they'll move on easily as they never had deep feelings about the relationship they were having with you in the first place. They'll also make sure you know how easy it is for them to move on.

If they decide to break up with you, it's likely that they already have a new source of supply who they want to take your place. Don't be surprised to see photos of a new love interest on social media soon after the breakup, if you still have social media contact with them that is.

It can be complicated and painful to live with a narcissistic ex, especially if you have children together. Maintain your boundaries, and don't become overly involved with them. Go grey rock and keep all interactions objective and business-like. If you have children together, try to at least maintain a civil relationship for their sake.

Don't be too hard on yourself if you feel sad at the end of the relationship, even if you've realized what a horrible person your ex is. Even if you don't miss the person you ended up with, you're still allowed to grieve for the loss of a relationship with the person you thought your partner was. You could still have strong feelings for your partner from the love-bombing stage when you got together at the beginning.

The narcissist may also act out toward you. They could become verbally abusive, and even threaten to harm themselves or commit suicide if they feel they've been abandoned.

Taking Care of Your Mental Health

Besides cutting contact and avoiding social media after your breakup, you need to pay attention to your own mental health.

Start focusing more on your self-care, as you need to be kind to yourself during the recovery period. You've probably been so lost in your relationship while trying to keep the narcissist happy, that you've been spending little time on yourself.

Think about things you used to do before you had to spend all your time on the narcissist. This could be hobbies that take time such as drawing, painting, cooking, or playing certain sports. Maybe you also want to spend more time with friends and get back into socializing. The narcissist may have kept you away from your friends and family.

You need to connect or reconnect with supportive people with whom you can confide about what went wrong in your relationship, as this can help you clear your mind and get things off your chest. Recovery is easier and faster when you have supportive people on your side.

Whatever happens, don't take the narcissist's behavior personally. Narcissists are broken individuals and nothing they say or do really has anything to do with you.

When they insult you, and call you names, you need to accept that this behavior has nothing to do with you. Just stay calm and don't take their insults seriously.

You need to let go of the need to get approval from the narcissist, as this will also make it easier to emotionally detach from them.

Recovering From PTSD

It's entirely possible to develop PTSD after prolonged mental and even physical abuse by a narcissist.

Narcissistic abuse such as belittling, manipulation, gaslighting, and devaluation could have had a significant impact on your self-worth and self-esteem. You may have become fearful, hypervigilant, and even numb. You could also feel ashamed and guilty, and experience symptoms such as flashbacks and intrusive memories.

This could also affect your relationships with others, and you may struggle to set healthy boundaries. If you're still with the narcissist, you may be walking on eggshells, because you don't want to trigger her and set off her anger.

Changes to the brain can occur, if someone is subject to long-term abuse. This could cause you to experience problems with concentration, memory, and controlling your emotions. You could also struggle to focus and make decisions. Your sleep can also be affected, as rumination about the abuse could cause you to struggle to fall and stay asleep.

What can make it even more difficult to handle this type of stress is that memories of trauma are easily triggered and could cause reactions such as flashbacks or panic attacks.

If you suffer from PTSD, you need to remember that this isn't a sign of weakness but that your brain is struggling to deal with the stress that the narcissist has caused you. The stress could still be ongoing, especially if you're in the process of getting divorced and there are children involved.

You could be feeling vulnerable after the breakup and you need to create a safe environment for yourself in which you can recover. Set boundaries for interacting with others that determine how they should interact with you. Remember that people often treat you in the way you treat yourself. Also cut contact with your narcissistic partner, if possible.

A good mental healthcare practitioner can help you overcome your trauma. Make sure you find one that has experience with narcissistic abuse so they can give you the best advice on how to deal with it.

Good self-care can also do wonders to improve your mood and reduce your stress levels. Keep a journal to track your progress and write down whatever you want to get the whole experience out of your system. Take part in enjoyable activities such as hobbies and sports, and visit people you may not have seen in a long time.

This will boost your mood. Also pay attention to your physical health by eating well, sleeping enough, and doing some exercise. If you have been neglecting these aspects of your life such as following an unhealthy diet or not exercising anymore, now is the time to be good to yourself and make some much-needed changes.

To give you more self-confidence and boost your self-esteem, it's also a good idea to focus on your personal growth. Set some new goals for yourself and consider if there is anything new you would like to learn to do. To distract yourself from the past drama you had in your life, you may even decide to take on new challenges.

You need to take it one day at a time. Remember that your healing will take time, so you need to be kind to yourself.

A Victim of Narcissistic Hoovering: Jack's Story

Jack met a woman named Sarah through a dating app. This woman at first appeared to be exceptionally charming and charismatic. In the early stages of their relationship, Sarah would often bring gifts for Jack's two daughters. Little did Jack know that Sarah was a narcissist and he was being groomed to be her primary source of supply. Sarah would tell Jack how badly her exes and her own family treated her. In these stories of woe, it was never Sarah's fault but everyone else's.

Jack fell for her sob stories and believed everything she said. He couldn't understand how people could be so horrible to such a lovely, kind, and caring woman. Sarah would ask Jack about his interests, and, lo and behold, she also shared the same interests. Jack had been captivated by Sarah's victim persona and by her use of mirroring.

Although he adored Sarah, Jack's intuition was telling him something was off, but he ignored his gut feeling and made excuses for her. Over time, Sarah started to devalue Jack. She would put him down with sarcastic comments and then claim she was just playing around and that he shouldn't be so sensitive. Sarah expected Jack to do what she wanted and if he said no she would display an array of passive-aggressive behaviors. She even acted in aggressive ways by slamming doors and shouting.

Jack started to suffer from cognitive dissonance and wondered what had happened to the lovely, kind, and caring woman she had been when they first met. Who was Sarah really? Jack distanced himself from Sarah, but she then used her children as pawns. Her children enjoyed spending time with Jack and his children and Sarah knew that Jack would find it difficult to say no if she made plans for them.

Sarah felt confident that she had Jack in her grasp and could do whatever she liked. She decided to treat him really well and took him out for nice meals and bought him clothes. Suddenly, without any warning, Sarah disappeared and didn't communicate. Jack asked her what was wrong and Sarah said she thought she needed some space, but she wasn't sure. Jack didn't like how this felt and didn't want to be in limbo waiting for Sarah to make up her mind. He used the opportunity to end the relationship and finally get away from Sarah.

Six months later, Sarah sent Jack an email saying she was going to change her children's schools. She was moving her children to the school that Jack's children attended. Jack responded as he wanted to keep things amicable if he was going to see Sarah daily at the school. Sarah started buying treats like sweets and ice cream for Jack's children again.

She called Jack and invited him out to the pub as "friends." Jack's close friends warned him about letting this woman back into his life. They knew she was a manipulator and they didn't want to see Jack get hurt again. Unfortunately, Jack ignored his friends and continued to spend more time with Sarah. Sarah love bombed Jack and ignored his boundaries.

When Jack said no, Sarah would just guilt-trip him into doing what she wanted. She eventually got Jack to be intimate with her again after a night at the pub. Jack realized immediately that it was a mistake and tried to tell Sarah the next day that they should only be friends. Sarah took this as a huge rejection.

Sarah became mean and told Jack she was going to tell people who he really was and she started a smear campaign against him. She started with Jack's close friends, Amy and Tom. Amy and Tom had known Jack for a long time and they didn't buy into Sarah's smear campaign. They distanced themselves from Sarah as they thought she was a troublemaker. Sarah managed to cause some drama but it was minimal. Jack didn't react to the smear campaign and it quickly faded away.

The moral of Jack's story is to never entertain a hoover from your covert female narcissist. Keep a strict no-contact regime. This means you should not engage with the narcissist at all. Do not go past their home and do not look at their social media. Block their phone number, email address, and any other way they have of contacting you. Do not go to places you know the narcissist goes to.

You need to stay no-contact in order to break the trauma bond. If you accept a hoover, then you set yourself back to square one in the healing process. You'll just be abused all over again. If you have children with a covert female narcissist implement the grey rock method.

Journaling Activity for Narcissistic Abuse Recovery

Journaling is an excellent way to recover from narcissistic abuse.

Sit somewhere you won't be interrupted, and make sure you have your journal or your computer/electronic device handy. If you're going to be keeping your journal entries on paper, it's best to buy a journal if you want to look back on your progress. Loose pages may just end up getting lost.

Now write about the following:

- Describe what you experienced in an honest and straightforward way. How did it make you feel, and how has it affected your self-esteem?
- Consider if the abuse has given you any negative thoughts about yourself, and write them down. How can you reframe these thoughts in a positive way?
- Describe changes you would like to make in your new life going forward. Do you want to pursue new goals and interests; for example, starting your own business?
- Write down some positive affirmations for yourself that you repeat daily. You can also put them up on the walls of your house so that you're reminded regularly of them. This can be anything from "I am competent" to "I can do this."

Key Takeaways

- The first step you need to take as part of your recovery process is to realize the relationship needs to end for the sake of your health.
- The time you've spent with your covert narcissistic partner could have caused significant emotional damage and you need time to recover.
- The relationship could have left you feeling unloved and unvalued.
- Your partner may have manipulated you to the extent that you lost your own identity and your self-esteem was damaged.
- Be prepared for the fallout when you end a relationship with a narcissist, as they will likely blame the breakup on you.
- She could try to convince you to come back or guilt-trip you into staying.
- The narcissist may also try to start smear campaigns against you.
- They can try to use hoovering techniques to pull you back into the relationship. They can love bomb you and tell you they're willing to reform. They could also play the victim and try to get you to feel sorry for leaving them.
- Some narcissists will try to draw you back in by "future faking." They make promises and plans for the future that they never keep.
- When it comes to dealing with a former narcissistic partner, the best technique to deal with them is to go "grey rock." This means making yourself

emotionally as uninteresting and unresponsive as possible to the narcissist.

- It's important to take care of your mental health after breaking up with a narcissist.
- Take care of yourself and do things that you enjoy, and visit people you couldn't see while you were still involved with the narcissist.
- Don't take the narcissist's behavior seriously, as nothing they say or do has anything to do with you.
- It's possible to develop PTSD after long-term abuse by a narcissist. You could experience all kinds of unpleasant symptoms such as flashbacks and intrusive thoughts.

A mental healthcare practitioner can help you learn techniques to deal with your trauma.

Chapter 4
Healing and Moving On

It's difficult and stressful to have a relationship with a narcissist. Narcissists can't love anyone as they don't even love themselves. They don't see you as a separate person with your own emotional needs but simply as someone who is there to satisfy all their needs—and give them the attention they so desperately crave.

They can be mean and vindictive in a bid to maintain control over you. Sometimes, you're scared to be around them, and you walk on eggshells, not to set off another fit of narcissistic rage.

Unfortunately, this can be extremely damaging emotionally, especially if you have to deal with it over an extended period.

If you manage to walk away from the narcissist, healing can be a long process that takes place in stages.

Healing Stages After Narcissistic Abuse

You've probably survived a range of abuse from the covert narcissist in your life—anything from gaslighting to abuse by proxy. Maybe you even feel you were to blame for some of the abuse you received. You could also be ashamed of the way you allowed your abuser to treat you. The truth is, constant abuse would have damaged your self-confidence and could even have led to a loss of identity. You could even be suffering from PTSD with flashbacks and intrusive thoughts.

There is no easy way to recover from narcissistic abuse, but you can do so in stages.

After you've physically escaped your situation with the narcissist by ending the relationship, you'll probably be in denial. You might tell yourself that what happened wasn't as bad as you initially thought and that you're just being overly sensitive. You might also wonder if there's anything you could have done to have prevented the abuse or if you could get her to change. Be careful of these thoughts, as the narcissist may also promise you that she's going to change, which will never happen. You also can't control someone else's behavior.

However, to be able to continue the healing process and to set boundaries to make sure it doesn't continue, you need to accept that you were in an abusive situation. This could take a long time if you were extensively manipulated by the narcissist that you always accept their version of events. If the narcissist is also using hoovering behavior in an attempt to lure you back into the relationship, this could add to your initial denial, as they might be treating you with affection and promising that they will change.

Once you've recognized and accepted your reality, you might become furious. You could be angry not only at the narcissist and yourself but also at everyone around you. You need to work through your anger to be able to move further along with your recovery. It's perfectly fine and healthy to feel angry about what you had to suffer, but holding onto this anger might mean that you will take longer to heal, or you might never entirely heal from your ordeal.

You need to find ways to express your anger in a healthy way and in a safe environment. Writing in a journal can help you express some of the negative emotions, and you should talk to a therapist if you feel the need to do so. Doing exercise and sports can also help you release anger in a healthy way.

When you realize what happened and the relationship is finally over, you need to accept it and move on, you may start feeling sad and depressed. It's important to feel all your emotions and talk to family or friends or a therapist if you feel the need to do so. Make sure you get the support that works for you, as it will help you not to become trapped in negative emotions.

When you accept what has happened, you can begin to fully focus on your recovery. You also need to be able to forgive yourself for putting up with the abuse. It would have worn down your confidence, and your self-talk would have become increasingly negative, which makes it especially difficult to get out of a relationship like this.

Think about what you would have said to a friend or family member in the same situation, forgive yourself, and let it go.

Eventually, you'll start being more positive and hopeful again about the future. You can rebuild your self-esteem and set boundaries against those who might have been toxic influences in your life. You'll find peace and happiness again, and your self-love will increase.

Narcissistic Abuse Therapy

Narcissistic abuse therapy can help you recover from the abuse if you feel you're not really getting better weeks or months after the relationship has ended. Therapy can help you understand what happened to you and why you're experiencing certain symptoms.

Now that you've decided to see a therapist, you need to find one who had experience in working with survivors of trauma or abuse and possibly also had experience in working with people with personality disorders. You should be comfortable working with this person.

You'll also have to figure out which types of therapy works best for you. Some people who survived narcissistic abuse find cognitive behavioral therapy (CBT) works best, while others prefer psychoanalytic or psychodynamic therapy.

CBT can help you identify and challenge negative thoughts and beliefs that you may have developed as a result of emotional abuse. This can include beliefs such as that you're unlovable or unworthy, and mistrusting others because you think they're out to get you in some way.

CBT can also help you develop coping skills to deal with the after-effects of the abuse. This can include strengthening your support network, improving your communication skills, and setting boundaries.

Schema therapy is particularly useful for survivors of narcissistic abuse. This therapy focuses on identifying and changing ingrained thoughts and behaviors, which are known as schemas that can contribute to the development of mental health problems. This therapy can help you identify and challenge schemas that may have developed as a result of the abuse, such as believing you're worthless.

Psychoanalytic therapy can help you determine the underlying psychological factors that could have led to you becoming involved in an abusive relationship. The therapist can also work with you to explore your early experiences when it comes to attachment and relationships, as well as your current patterns of behavior and emotional responses. The therapist will help you work through unresolved issues from your past that could be contributing to your current struggles.

Object relations therapy is a form of psychoanalytic therapy that can help you deal with the narcissistic abuse you experienced. It will help you explore your internalized representation of yourself and others, that you could have developed as a result of your early attachment experiences. The therapy can also help you explore how the abuse affected your self-concept and your relationship with others. Understanding this can help you work toward developing healthier relationships in the future.

This type of therapy can take time, but if you're struggling to move forward, psychoanalytic therapy can help you find deep and lasting healing.

Psychodynamic therapy can also help you understand how your abusive relationship could have impacted your sense of self and your ability to form a healthy relationship. You'll have to develop a close working relationship with your therapist and this will help you explore your thoughts and feelings in a safe environment. The therapist will help you identify patterns of behavior you could have developed as a result of the abuse and will also help you find healthier ways of relating to others.

Self-psychology is a form of psychodynamic therapy that can be useful for people who have experienced narcissistic abuse. It focuses on your internal sense of self, and how it might have been damaged by the abusive relationship. You can then work toward rebuilding a healthier self-concept.

Why You Shouldn't Feel Sorry for the Narcissist

It can be tempting to feel empathy and compassion for a narcissist, as most people who have this personality disorder had a rough start in life. It's often abuse and neglect which caused them to develop the personality disorder. It's a coping mechanism, as nobody protected them in childhood.

However, while their past can explain their current abusive behavior, it's not a justification for the horrific way they treat others in adulthood.

Unfortunately, they are unlikely to think about how they are hurting others, as their emotions are shallow and they will usually disappear from relationships when people stop meeting their needs.

When you leave your abusive relationship, you may feel terrible for leaving your ex-partner behind, who probably had already experienced abuse and mistreatment in her life, but you do need to set boundaries to protect yourself. While it's normal to feel empathy for them, they have no right to hurt you because they were hurt in the past. As adults, they have agency and the capacity to find the help they need.

They can get therapy or other forms of help, and they may have refused to do so. Some may also start therapy and then drop out soon because they refuse to change. They often think that they're perfectly fine and that you're the "crazy" one with the problem. They will also tell you so.

Understanding narcissism can help you coexist with them. A narcissist may want you back after ending the relationship. This is not because they are heartbroken and regret losing you as a person, and that they care about how you feel, but rather because they see you as one of their favorite possessions that they've lost. Another reason a narcissist will try to get back with you is just to punish you and then be the one to discard you if you left them first.

When they get you back, they won't act differently in the long run, and you'll soon find out that they haven't changed at all. They might just miss you because now they don't have someone to run after them and meet all their needs. They could just miss something they no longer have and that used to keep them entertained before; for example, almost like a broken TV set or a computer game.

Another reason why you shouldn't feel sorry for a narcissist is because they don't have empathy for anyone and they genuinely don't care how anyone else around them feels.

They're also incapable of reflecting on their own bad behavior and if they think about anything to do with their behavior, it's usually just about their self-interest. If they tell you they love you, it's more about them loving what you can do for them.

Narcissists also know what they're doing when they're manipulating you and hurting your feelings; however, they just don't care. They won't even have empathy when you become emotional or cry, and they may accuse you of being overdramatic while enjoying your suffering. They will even turn the situation around on you, and make it your own fault that you've been hurt.

Whether you leave them, or they decide to leave you in the end, tell yourself that you should be grateful to have this person out of your life, and that you've dodged a bullet. There is nothing you can do for them, and you can't help them to change. Narcissists never change, and living with them is just a lifelong drama series.

Post-Traumatic Growth

Post-traumatic growth (PTG) refers to the positive changes that can happen in your life as the result of a traumatic event you experienced. It's challenging to cope with trauma; however, some people may experience growth in a number of areas, such as personal relationships, spirituality, and resilience. Everyone will also experience it in a different way.

Some people do experience PTG after narcissistic abuse if they have the right support, but this isn't guaranteed.

After breaking free from your abusive relationship and healing, you may experience growth in the following areas:

- You could have gained a better understanding of yourself and your needs. Being involved with an abusive and manipulative person could have caused you to question your identity, values, and beliefs.

- You could have become more attuned to the suffering of others, which means you'll be more empathetic toward them. In general, you could become a more compassionate and empathetic person. You could have become closer to certain people in your life.
- You could become a more resilient person during the recovery process and learn better coping skills. You realize you're stronger than you thought, and you're able to handle what life throws at you.
- You may have seen new possibilities in life and you appreciate life in ways you never had before.

How to Set Healthy Boundaries in Your Future Relationships

Now that you've ended your relationship with a narcissist, and you're ready to move on, it's important that you know how to set healthy boundaries in your future relationships. You don't want to find yourself in a similar toxic situation ever again, and as the old adage says, "Other people will treat you as you treat yourself."

Healthy boundaries help us to treat others with mutual respect in relationships.

A couple in a healthy relationship both have strong self-esteem, and they feel free to assert their boundaries with their partners and also act vulnerable. They're not constantly attached to their partners and they're free to think and act independently.

If you know your partner, you can also understand them better as people. If you respect their limits, they'll feel safer opening up to you, and you'll be able to form an even more intimate connection.

Relationship Boundaries

Relationships require different kinds of boundaries.

Emotional boundaries help you to have empathy for the other person without absorbing their emotions. It's vital to remember that you control your emotional well-being, regardless of what the other person in the relationship might be feeling. Establishing emotional boundaries is about retaining our individuality, while still caring about the other person in the relationship.

We all have different boundaries when it comes to physical intimacy and sex. It's important that you discuss what type of contact you prefer so that you can have a trusting and respectful relationship.

Financial boundaries can bring about some tough conversations in relationships. You need to decide what your financial goals are and set your relationship boundaries accordingly. For example, decide how much you're willing to spend on gifts for each other or what you're willing to spend during your social excursions.

Intellectual boundaries and respecting each other's different viewpoints are also important in a relationship. Your partner won't be able to share all your opinions and viewpoints, and you should be able to share your different views without fighting.

Setting intellectual boundaries also allows you to be true to yourself and your opinions.

An example of a healthy relationship boundary is to expect your partner to communicate with maturity during disagreements and to leave situations when you feel they're not communicating respectfully.

The success of most relationships depends on healthy boundaries, as they help maintain a balance between you and your partner. They minimize conflict because you know what to expect from each other. Boundaries will also help you communicate honestly about what you need. You also need to listen to your partner and what their needs are. You need to discuss their boundaries and why it's important to them.

In healthy relationships, there should be respect from both sides. Communicating with compassion, respect, and understanding will ensure that you have a better relationship in the long term.

Ending your relationship with a female covert narcissist will give you the opportunity to lead a healthier and more fulfilling life. Once you've started the healing process and you've addressed the emotional and psychological impact of the abuse you've suffered, you can learn how to identify and avoid unhealthy relationships in the future.

If you learn how to set and enforce healthy boundaries, and you improve your self-esteem, as well as express your emotions in healthy and constructive ways, you'll be able to have healthier and more fulfilling relationships.

Healing From Narcissistic Abuse: Shaun's Story

Shaun has always been eager to make everyone around him happy, and his friends and family knew he would always be willing to help them out.

When he met Stella, he fell head-over-heels in love with the charismatic woman. She gave him lots of attention and affection, and he did anything he could to please her.

However, as their relationship continued, Shaun noticed that Stella's behavior had started changing, and it wasn't for the better.

She became extremely controlling and manipulated him into doing things he didn't want to do. She also guilt-tripped him when he didn't meet her demands, and would often explode into a rage. He felt like he had to walk on eggshells when he was with her, as he never knew what would make her explode in anger.

After talking to a psychologist friend and reading some books, Shaun realized Stella was a covert narcissist. He finally couldn't take it any longer and ended the relationship, but he realized healing would take time.

He realized that he first had to acknowledge and accept what happened. He read as much as possible about this type of emotional abuse and how it could affect a person's self-esteem. Talking to other people who had similar experiences made him feel less alone.

Next, he had to set some boundaries. He realized that he had to say "no" and prioritize his own needs; otherwise, others would just take advantage of him. He also started to recognize narcissistic behavior which helped him a lot when it came to avoiding these types of relationships in the future.

He also started rebuilding his self-esteem and focused on learning to appreciate himself for who he was, rather than looking for approval from other people. Shaun also started practicing better self-care, which involved doing exercise regularly and developing better eating habits. It took him a while to appreciate that he needed to take time to care for himself, but eventually, he felt better physically and mentally just from following a healthier lifestyle.

Shaun regained his joy in life as he also started spending time on hobbies and people Stella didn't approve of when they were still together. The healing process was difficult, but he emerged as a stronger person, with more confidence. He also learned valuable lessons about healthy boundaries in relationships and what warning signs to watch out for when becoming involved with someone.

Activities: Boundary-Setting Exercise

Find somewhere quiet to sit and write down your thoughts in your journal or type them on your laptop or any other electronic devices you may use.

Consider the following:

- Write your boundaries down, and look at them regularly. Think about them as you navigate your relationship.
- Also, communicate your boundaries to your partner in a respectful way.
- Ask your partner to communicate their boundaries to you. Listen to their needs and what they prefer, and respect them. This will help you build a stronger relationship.
- Once you've set your boundaries, you need to practice setting them. Communicate with your partner if they do anything to violate your boundaries.

- Think about your progress when it comes to setting boundaries and if you're starting to feel more empowered. Is it helping you and your partner to communicate more effectively?

Finally, setting boundaries is an ongoing process and you're going to have to be patient with yourself and your partner.

Key Takeaways

- A narcissist can't love anyone, as they don't love themselves.
- They regard people in their life as simply being there to satisfy their needs and give them the attention they desperately crave.
- You may feel that you are to blame for the abuse you received from the narcissist and for the way in which you allowed yourself to be treated.
- Constant abuse would have damaged your self-esteem and could have led to a loss of identity.
- You might be in denial and tell yourself that the abuse you suffered wasn't that bad and that you were simply in denial.
- To be able to heal, you need to accept that you were in an abusive situation.
- Once you accept what happened, you might feel a lot of anger.
- You need to find appropriate ways to deal with your anger; otherwise, it will take you longer to heal or you may never heal entirely.

- Narcissistic abuse therapy can help you recover, especially if you feel you're not really getting better sometime after the relationship has ended.
- You need to find a therapist who has experience in working with survivors of trauma and abuse, as well as people with personality disorders.
- You need to find out which types of therapy work best for you. You could benefit from CBT, psychoanalytic, or psychodynamic therapy.
- CBT can help you identify and challenge negative beliefs and thoughts you may have developed as a result of emotional abuse.
- Schema therapy is a type of CBT that focuses on identifying and changing ingrained thoughts and behaviors.
- Psychoanalytic therapy can help you understand the underlying psychological factors that could have caused you to become involved in an abusive relationship.
- Object relations therapy can help you explore your internalized representation of yourself and others.
- Psychodynamic therapy can help you understand how your abusive relationship affected your self-esteem, and your ability to form a healthy relationship.
- Self-psychology can help you rebuild a healthier self-concept.
- PTG refers to positive changes that can happen in your life after the trauma you experienced.
- Some people may experience PTG after a traumatic relationship, but this isn't guaranteed.

- If you develop better coping skills, you could be a more resilient person after the end of your abusive relationship.
- You'll also have become a more empathetic person who understands other people better.
- Healthy relationships require different kinds of boundaries.
- Emotional boundaries mean you can be empathetic toward people without accepting responsibility for their emotions.
- Setting boundaries means you can be true to yourself and your views.
- In a healthy relationship, the partners are able to share viewpoints without fighting.
- You and your partner should be able to communicate with maturity during disagreements.

Chapter 5
Moving Forward and Living Your Best Life

The best thing you can do after getting out of an abusive relationship is not to jump right back into another relationship, but to spend time on yourself, and find new purpose and meaning in your life.

Maybe this is the first time in your life that you're actually prioritizing yourself and your own needs. If you've been conditioned since childhood to please others and live up to their expectations, this could be a completely new phase of life for you.

This can be a confusing time as well, especially if you're not used to being alone and have been part of a couple for most of your adult life. So, how do you go ahead, make changes, and live your best life?

The truth is, this is the best opportunity you'll get for personal growth that can take you to the next level when it comes to your life. Now is the time to forge a new path for your life.

Focusing on Personal Growth

Planning, motivation, and hard work are all important when it comes to personal growth. However, first, you need to find purpose and meaning in life.

Don't feel pressured to rush headlong into all kinds of self-improvement projects, now that you have time for yourself. You may want to distract yourself from your failed relationship as much as possible, but if you tend toward perfectionistic overachieving, it can be tempting to become obsessed about another area of your life instead of spending more time on self-care and living a healthy, balanced lifestyle. That's why it's important to first take the time to consider what's really important to you.

The way to go is to find projects that will make you happy. Try to focus on a few things at the same time; for example, change your diet to eat healthier, start working out, and start a side hustle to supplement your income. It's tempting to put all your energy into one project such as starting an online business, and then spend all hours working on this to fill the gap in your life that was left by the failed relationship. Rather focusing on different things will change the way you think and will help you rebuild your self-esteem and increase your resilience.

Make sure you do fun things as well, such as taking an evening off to watch movies that you enjoy, but didn't get around to watching when you were with your ex, reading books you enjoy, or going for long walks.

Finding New Purpose

It can be difficult to find a new sense of purpose when you're coming out of an abusive relationship, but it's possible.

Consider your values and what's important to you. What are your interests and strengths? What types of activities fulfill you?

You also need to set some goals for yourself to get motivated. These can be short- and long-term goals, and they can be for any aspect of your life, whether it's personal, professional, or social. If you can achieve your goals, it will boost your confidence and give you a sense of confidence.

It may take you some time to find your purpose, so don't be upset if you end up feeling stuck for a while and you don't start making progress immediately. It's a sign of progress if you start doing things, even if you fail a few times, and have to try something else or try again.

Maybe you feel like you've been working hard but you're not really getting anywhere. You were initially ambitious about where you were going, but your toxic and emotionally draining relationship made you lose focus on your career and the rest of your life.

A proper goal-setting technique can get you back on track.

Setting Goals

It can be difficult to focus on setting goals, especially when you're still distracted by what happened to you in the past. However, there are techniques like the SMART goal-setting technique that can make setting goals and achieving them much easier.

SMART goals are a framework that can help you set goals and objectives that you can measure and which are relevant and achievable.

Each letter in the acronym, SMART, represents a step in the goal-setting process:

- **Specific:** Your goals need to be clear, as well as what you need to do to achieve them. You must also understand why they're important to you.
- **Measurable:** You should be able to measure your goals so that you know how far you are from achieving them. This should also allow you to see where you need to make changes that will enable you to achieve your goals.
- **Achievable:** The goals you set for yourself should be achievable. You need to think of obstacles and challenges you need to overcome. Your goals should be challenging, but they shouldn't be so difficult that they end up overwhelming you.
- **Relevant:** Your values and goals should be relevant to your overall priorities and objectives.
- **Time-bound:** You should have a timeframe for your goals and should be able to monitor your progress. It will also make you work harder toward achieving your goals if there is a timeframe attached to them.

SMART Goal-Setting Explained

Expanding on the acronym will give you a clearer idea of the goal-setting process.

Specific

When it comes to making your goal specific, you should consider the following questions:

- What is it that you want to achieve?
- Why is it important to you?
- What resources will you need?
- Who is involved?
- Does it involve a specific place?

Example: I want to start my own online business to boost my cash flow and my career in general. I need access to the internet and I will have to do courses to improve my knowledge.

Measurable

You should be able to track your progress and measure your goals. This will help you stay focused and get excited about meeting them.

When it comes to measuring your goals, you'll have to ask yourself how you will know when you have achieved your goals.

Example: Which steps have you taken in starting your business? Have you taken courses to improve your skills? Have you started doing freelance work?

Achievable

Your goal must be realistic, and you should in some way be able to achieve it. While it should be challenging, it should not be so difficult that it's unlikely that you will be able to achieve it.

Think about how you can accomplish your goal. Is your goal realistic, based on the constraints that you face?

Example: You've decided you want to follow a new career, for example, you want to become a psychologist. However, you're already 35 years old and in a fairly lucrative career that you actually enjoy. You also have children who need your attention and financial support. This would be a complete career change for you, which would mean you would first need to study to get the relevant degrees.

Before you go ahead, ask yourself if you will really have the time for all the studying that will be required. Can you afford to do this financially? It could mean a few years of not working, or only being able to work part-time. Would you still be able to support your children and spend time with them?

Relevant

You need to make sure that this goal is really important to you.

You can ask yourself the following questions, to make sure that this is really what you want:

- Does this goal seem worthwhile to you and is it the right time to try and achieve it?
- Are you the right person to be going after this goal?
- Is this goal applicable in the current socioeconomic environment?

Example: Is it really the right time for you to study, and can you afford it? Don't you perhaps already have too many commitments?

Time-Bound

Your goals need target dates so that you can focus on working towards the deadlines. This will prevent everyday tasks from overwhelming your long-term goals.

Think in terms of what you can do today, several weeks from now, and then several months from now.

Example:

- How long will it take you to get the skills you need for a new career?
- Will you need more training, and what would be a realistic time frame for this?

How Volunteering Makes You Feel Better About Yourself

Volunteering is also a great way to move on from your own troubles. You're helping others while connecting with new people, making friends, learning new skills, and even advancing your career.

Helping others can boost your mental health by reducing stress and depression and giving you a new sense of purpose.

You'll get the chance to boost your social skills and make new friends. A meaningful connection to other people will relieve your stress levels. Working with animals can also improve your mood and relieve your anxiety.

Volunteering can also increase your self-confidence. It gives you a sense of accomplishment to help others around you, and if you feel better about yourself, you're more likely to have a positive outlook on life.

It could also give you the skills you need if you want to make a career change. It's also a way of trying out a new career before you take definite steps to find a new job.

So, how do you start volunteering?

Before you start volunteering, you should consider your interests and what you really enjoy doing. Are you looking for something to do as a hobby, or are you looking for a potential new career?

One of the best ways to begin is to visit different organizations and see if you get along with the staff and other volunteers. These could include anything from a youth organization to your local Lions Club.

Volunteer as much time as you feel comfortable with, and keep it fun. If it takes too much of your time, it just becomes another stress factor in your life, especially if you have a busy career as well.

Building Resilience After a Toxic Relationship

In simple terms, resilience is the ability to bounce back from difficult events and disappointments in your life. You have the ability to deal with setbacks and stressors and move on. You also have the ability to deal with challenges and learn and grow from them.

You have two choices after a failed relationship: accept that it's over, heal, and move on with your life. The other alternative is to become depressed, and even run back to an abusive relationship.

It's possible to build resilience during your healing journey. It's not a special skill or personality trait. In fact, anyone can learn how to be resilient.

If you've been through an abusive relationship, you've got the potential to bounce back.

Firstly, you've got to accept that it happened to you and that you haven't got the power to go back and change anything. It doesn't help to use your energy to fight against something that already happened and give it more airtime than it deserves. You have a limited amount of energy and you need to invest it into positive people and things.

You need to take care of yourself and boost your self-esteem. Your toxic relationship may have left you feeling that you're not worthy of love.

When you practice self-care your brain will believe you are worthy of love, which will also help when it comes to building resilience.

You need to overcome the negative thinking you may have become accustomed to as a result of the abuse you experienced. If you want to be more resilient, you need to learn to think optimistic thoughts.

You can do this in the following way. First, consider what you think, and why you're thinking in this way.

- Who/what is the problem?: "My wife screams at me and manipulates me."

- What do you believe about the person or the situation?: "She treats me in this way because I messed up and I don't deserve love. I deserve to be treated in this way."
- What are the consequences of your thinking in this way?: "I'm scared to start new relationships because I don't believe in myself."
- Reframe your thoughts in a more positive light.
- Ask yourself if you can really be responsible for another adult's behavior or if they should be able to manage their own behavior and actions. One person mistreated you, but many others love and respect you. Does this not show that you're worthy of love and care?
- A supportive social circle can also play an important role in you becoming more resilient. You need to surround yourself with supportive people who you can talk to if you need to do so.
- You can be negative about life in general after suffering through an abusive relationship. Gratitude can help you dispel some of this negativity. Writing in a journal can help you cultivate gratitude; write down a list of things you have to be grateful for at the end of every day. It could be simple things, such as having a roof over your head or having nutritious food to eat. Or you could be grateful for simple, everyday activities, such as going to lunch with a friend.
- If you train yourself to look for the positive things around you, you'll gradually become more grateful and positive. This will help you to be more resilient and stronger, even in tough times.

- As a resilient person, you need to take back control over your life and how your story is going to play out. You didn't cause the abuse you suffered in your relationship.

Finally, once you've developed a more positive mindset, you need to start dreaming again for the future and find a way to make your dreams come true. After all, this is your second chance for a happy and successful life, and you want to make the most of it.

Finding a New Purpose in Life: Sam's Story

Sam's girlfriend Lucy used to belittle him in front of his friends and family, criticized his choices, and made fun of his interests. She manipulated him into doing things she wanted and visiting people she wanted to visit, but he didn't. She also guilt-tripped him when he didn't do what she wanted him to do.

As time passed, he realized that Lucy was a covert narcissist and that he had been in an abusive relationship for years.

Sam decided to leave her and started to rediscover himself and what was truly important to him. He went for trips on his motorcycle, something Lucy didn't allow him to do because she said it was too dangerous. He also started reading and drawing again, activities Lucy also criticized because she said it was a waste of time and he could be doing something more useful with his time, like taking her to the shops.

Sam found a new purpose in his life the more he started doing things on his own. He volunteered at an animal shelter and found it fulfilled him in a new way that he hasn't experienced before.

He also went to therapy where he learned new ways to have healthy relationships and how to cope with his emotions. He started to see the world in a new, more positive way.

Journaling Activity: Create a Personal Growth Plan

A personal growth plan can help you identify your strengths and weaknesses and set your goals for your future life. This can also help you continue your healing journey.

The easiest way is to create your growth plan in your journal. This can be on paper or on an electronic device.

- Think about how your relationship with the female covert narcissist has impacted you positively and negatively. Write all your thoughts down in your journal.
- Write down your strengths and weaknesses. Think about anything that might hold you back on your future journey. If you're not too sure what your good points are, ask your friends and family for feedback.
- Think about your purpose, and what you want to achieve. Set goals using the SMART technique discussed in this chapter.
- Make sure you have action steps for your goals. Write down the specific steps you'll take for every goal.
- Create a timeline for your goals and create smaller milestones.
- Keep track of your progress toward reaching your goals.

- Take it one day at a time, and remember that it's a process to achieve your goals. Don't put too much pressure on yourself if you miss milestones. Just keep going and get back on track.

Key Takeaways

- After exiting an abusive relationship, you need to spend time finding a new purpose and meaning in your life.
- It's the perfect opportunity to work on finding a new life path.
- You also shouldn't feel pressured to start self-improvement projects.
- You need to take time to consider what is important to you and what you really want to do.
- Spend your time on activities that will build your self-esteem and increase your resilience.
- Make time to do fun things as well.
- When you've decided on a purpose, you can decide on goals for your new phase of life.
- A goal-setting technique such as SMART can help you get on the right track when it comes to setting goals.
- SMART is about setting specific, measurable, achievable, relevant, and time-bound goals.
- Volunteering can increase your self-confidence and help you make new social connections. It's also a good way of getting a new perspective on your own troubles.
- Resilience is the ability to bounce back from difficulties in your life such as a failed relationship.

Anyone can learn and build resilience. It's not a special skill or personality trait.

Chapter 6
Helping Others and Raising Awareness

You might prefer to heal in private from the narcissistic abuse you suffered, which is perfectly fine. However, it's also possible to enhance your healing and help others by sharing your experiences with them.

Narcissistic abuse can be isolating and confusing since the manipulation that is involved might cause you to doubt your own experiences. Knowing that others have had a similar experience might help people at least not to feel alone during their healing process.

Sharing your experience can also help others to gain insight into the behavior of a narcissist and the type of abuse they inflict on people. It can also help break down the stigma surrounding narcissistic abuse. Speaking out can raise awareness and understanding.

You can also be empowered by sharing your experiences with others. You can encourage them to seek help and escape their abusive situation.

Sharing Your Story

It can be a nerve-wracking experience to share your story with other people. Many abuse survivors also fear judgment, as there is a tendency, especially on social media, to dismiss anyone who speaks out about something as being an attention seeker.

You could also fear being seen as weak and needy. In a world where we refer to people as "snowflakes" if they're struggling to deal with something, you may be told that you're just thin-skinned and that you've got to get used to the way the world works. If you didn't suffer physical abuse, your experience may also be dismissed as not being as bad as that of someone else.

You could also have the fear that others simply won't believe you. Narcissistic abuse is often so strange and manipulative that others may struggle to believe you when you tell them about it. For example, it might be very difficult for someone to believe that a narcissist can fly into a rage about small things.

Narcissists are also adept at the way they present their false personas to the world. Others might find it almost impossible to believe that they are a completely different abusive person behind closed doors. Even people who have seen them behave in abusive ways but haven't been victims themselves may struggle to understand the extent of their abusive behavior.

Many people still don't have an understanding of psychology, and they may accuse you of labeling people, and consider it normal for some people to just have more "difficult" personalities than others. There may even be an expectation that you should feel sorry for the abuser, for experiences that she has suffered in the past, including in her childhood.

It's important to keep in mind that there will be people who act unfavorably when you share your story, especially if they're in some way connected to your narcissistic ex. You might even be accused of conducting a smear campaign, even if you don't mention her name, by the people who know you.

You may feel triggered by backlash or unfavorable words, but it's vital to remember that you can't control the reactions of other people. Just remember that you're in charge of your life, and it's up to you how you react to other people's words.

You could also be scared of reliving trauma when you tell your story. It can be a difficult experience that brings back painful memories.

Educating the Public About Covert Female Narcissism

Educating others about covert female narcissism and even narcissism in general, can help them protect themselves from becoming involved in potentially abusive relationships. However, keep in mind that NPD can only be diagnosed by qualified mental healthcare practitioners.

Someone could display narcissistic tendencies as a result of past trauma, being treated as special throughout their lives, and even societal norms that encourage self-promotion. People with some of these tendencies are still capable of displaying empathy and having healthy relationships, even if they could experience certain difficulties in their relationships.

However, education can also be useful for people with narcissistic tendencies as they need to gain awareness of how their behavior affects everyone around them. They can learn to develop empathy and a better understanding of those around them. Therapy can also help people with these traits to learn more about themselves and can assist them to effectively develop healthier relationships.

If you feel you want to educate the public about narcissism and create more awareness of what they need to look out for, you can do so in a number of ways.

You can create online resources, or ask someone else to create them for you. Useful awareness material can include website articles, blog posts, videos, or a podcast that can discuss the signs and symptoms of narcissism, and red flags you need to look out for when you're in a relationship. Social media content is an excellent way to reach people, and you can also use it to reinforce what you possibly could have said during a presentation or facts that were discussed during a meeting.

It's also possible to reach a large audience by sharing material via social media platforms and websites.

Holding workshops and seminars about this subject can also be a good way of educating the public. However, you might not enjoy public speaking or feel uncomfortable talking about what you went through face-to-face with people. However, you could share your experience with mental health professionals and advocacy groups that organize events like this, if you don't want to address people directly.

What is helpful about workshops is that they provide a safe space where people can share their experiences and learn from others. For example, you might find there are other survivors of narcissistic abuse who are willing to speak out about their experiences.

You could also share your story in the form of an interview with media outlets, such as magazines, websites, and other media platforms. For example, if any of these outlets do an interview with a mental health professional, they can interview you to get more information on people's real-life experiences with this type of abuse.

Educational awareness campaigns that include a lot of information are always a good option. However, it would probably be too expensive for you to do something like this on your own, and you would have to work with advocacy groups and mental health professionals to create educational campaigns about covert narcissism.

Effective campaigns will include a range of material; anything from printed posters, flyers, and guides, to social media hashtags.

Narcissistic Abuse Support Groups

A lot of awareness can also be created by means of narcissistic abuse support groups. This is a safe space where survivors of abuse get together to support each other, connect with others who also went through this, and share their experiences. Educational material can also be shared in support groups so that members can learn more about NPD, and what to do about the situation in which they find themselves.

Some of these groups will be led by members, and others might be managed by qualified psychotherapists. There are several different types of support groups, namely in-person, online, and even phone support groups.

Online and phone support groups provide you with the comfort to connect with others from your home. Taking part in a support group can play an important role in your healing journey.

How Can You Find a Support Group?

Domestic violence centers typically run support groups for survivors of intimate partner violence (IPV) and narcissistic abuse qualifies as a form of IPV.

Help Within Reach and I Believe Your Abuse are two organizations that offer helpful advice and resources. Help Within Reach offers abuse support groups virtually. The groups are open virtually regardless of their location.

If you want to join a support group, you need to find one that will suit your needs. You will need to consider some of the different characteristics of the groups:

- Do you want a structured or more informal group? Do you want a group with a specific focus or topic, or are you happy to go with a general group?
- Consider the size of the group. Are you happy to join a small, intimate group or would you prefer a larger group where you'll have more anonymity?
- Make sure that the group you join is led by a trained facilitator who has knowledge about the subject and can provide sufficient guidance and support.
- It's in your best interest to join a group that has some guidelines or rules that the participants are expected

to follow. Rules could be about maintaining confidentiality and respecting others.

- Is the group online or in a specific physical location? If you want a physical group, you'll want one that is conveniently located close to you.

Creating Change

There is still a stigma attached to men coming forward and admitting they've been emotionally abused. Society still clings to the adage: "Boys don't cry." However, it's vital to support those who have been abused by covert female narcissists and to create a safe environment in which they can heal from their experiences.

It's important to provide the survivors of narcissistic abuse with resources that can help them recover. This can include referrals to mental health professionals and support groups.

Advocacy groups can also raise awareness and provide educational resources.

Joining or supporting those groups that promote laws and regulations that protect victims of emotional abuse and domestic violence can also be an effective way of promoting change. These groups can also create awareness about the issue, and lobby for policy changes.

Some victims of narcissistic abuse could also need help to pursue legal action against their abusers. This can be a good way to hold abusers accountable, as they may get restraining orders or criminal charges can be filed against them and victims could possibly seek damages against them in civil court.

Educating and training mental health professionals, law enforcement, and the general public about narcissism is also a good way to promote change. This will make it less likely that victims of narcissistic abuse aren't believed or even ridiculed.

Ultimately, we can work toward creating a safer society by creating change and backing laws and regulations that hold abusers responsible for their deeds and safeguard abused people.

What Is the Difference Between NPD and Having Narcissistic Traits?

If you're not professionally qualified in mental health, it might be difficult to identify if you're involved with a covert narcissist, or simply someone with certain narcissistic traits. However, there are definite differences between the two.

Someone with NPD won't accept responsibility for their actions, while someone with narcissistic traits can recognize when they've hurt people and feel sorry about their behavior.

Someone who has narcissistic traits is unlikely to admit to their faults and they may object to constructive criticism but they have the capacity to deal with this, even if it's limited.

Some traits that appear narcissistic can be traced back to childhood insecurities. For example, someone who is always looking for compliments about their appearance or feels the need to brag after they achieved certain things. Someone could keep posting selfies on social media not because they're a narcissist, but because they're looking for attention that they're not getting in real life.

The main difference between a narcissist and someone with narcissistic tendencies is that someone who only exhibits certain tendencies, but hasn't actually been diagnosed with NPD, is capable of feeling empathy and usually treats their family and friends with kindness. They don't exploit others for their own gain like a narcissist.

Educating Others About Narcissism: Sam's Story

Sam had recently broken off his relationship with his girlfriend after he discovered she was a covert narcissist and he got tired of the demeaning way in which she treated him.

He noticed he felt better about his experiences after talking to others about it, and he decided that he wanted to educate other people about what he went through so that they could hopefully avoid the same damaging experience. Sam started by doing research. He read books and articles. He also talked to other survivors of narcissistic abuse. He learned more from other people's practical experiences with narcissists in their lives and the different types of control and manipulation they experienced.

He decided that he wanted to share his experience, so he started a blog based on his personal story and the lessons he learned. He updated the blog regularly and wrote articles about the red flags to watch out for when you suspect you're in a relationship with a narcissist. He also wrote about the recovery process, and how long it took him to move past this relationship.

Eventually, Sam also got the courage to speak at local events and support groups. He gave others hope and showed them healing was possible.

Sam eventually became an expert speaker on the topic of narcissistic abuse and he felt he was making a difference in the world. It felt good to turn his pain into purpose and to help others.

Activity: Write About Your Experience With Narcissistic Abuse

Pull your journal closer, and write a few paragraphs about your experience with narcissistic abuse. You can also type your story if that's more convenient for you. You can also create a timeline of the events that took place.

Write about how you first started your relationship with the narcissist and what attracted you to her.

Consider the behaviors you found abusive and how they made you feel. What was the impact of the abuse on your life?

Indicate if you looked for support while you were in the relationship and what the response you received from others was.

Write about where you are now at this stage of your life, and if your recovery was successful. What have you learned about yourself and narcissistic abuse?

Key Takeaways

- It can enhance your healing process to share your experiences with others who might also be experiencing narcissistic abuse.

- Narcissistic abuse can be isolating since the manipulation involved could make you doubt your experiences.
- Speaking out and raising awareness can also end the stigma surrounding narcissistic abuse.
- You might have certain fears about sharing your experiences, and that you possibly won't be believed.
- The narcissist is adept at presenting a false persona to the world, so it might be difficult for others to believe that they're a completely different person behind closed doors.
- Keep in mind that there will always be people who react unfavorably when you share your story.
- You might even be accused of starting a smear campaign against the narcissist.
- Educating others about narcissism might help them not to become involved in abusive relationships.
- Someone could also have narcissistic tendencies as a result of past trauma, and not necessarily be a narcissist.
- People who have narcissistic tendencies can still be empathetic and have healthy relationships, even though they may experience certain difficulties.
- You could benefit from joining a narcissistic support group.
- Narcissistic support groups are safe spaces where survivors of abuse can support each other.
- You can also join online and telephonic support groups from the comfort of your home.
- Advocacy groups can raise awareness about narcissistic abuse and provide educational resources.

Chapter 7
Narcissistic Parenting

If you share children with your narcissistic ex, you need some background on how narcissists deal with parenting, as well as how to coparent with a narcissist.

Parents play a major role in their children's lives until they eventually leave home. Children who grow up with narcissistic parents often struggle with self-esteem, and they have to shape themselves into what their parents wanted them to be.

Narcissists often view their children as extensions of themselves, although they might become completely detached or disinterested in their children once they become adults.

When their child becomes more autonomous, they ignore the child or treat them in a more overbearing way. They regard the child's independence as a threat to their carefully constructed false persona, and they may be afraid that the child will eventually even compete with them.

Children of narcissists can grow up with insecure codependent personalities, and in severe cases of abuse, might even suffer from PTSD. Some remember their childhoods as being weird and uncomfortable, and that they suffered from anxiety while growing up.

However, many people who suffered narcissistic abuse as children, still struggle to see it as such, especially when there was no physical abuse involved. They may have been expected to provide emotional validation and regulation to their parents, or they were *parentified* and had emotional problems dropped on them.

If a child has to take care of their parent's emotional and psychological needs, it's emotional abuse. Adults are supposed to be able to regulate their own emotions, and shouldn't be relying on their children to be their pacifiers.

The Narcissistic Mother

A narcissist will always put herself first, even to the detriment of her own children who depend on her for emotional support and their overall well-being.

She struggles with low self-esteem and shame and can be judgmental because of her entitlement. The world will always owe her more because life has been unfair to her.

Female covert narcissists often had narcissistic parents themselves, and their relationships in adulthood are distorted by their childhood experiences with narcissistic parents.

Narcissistic mothers raise their children in an emotionally damaging environment. They tend to see especially their daughters as personal reflections of themselves and could expect the children to be perfect in everything they do.

The covert narcissistic mother may see her child as an extension of herself. There are no boundaries between her and her children, and she is unable to see her children as individuals in their own right. She has a rigid way of thinking and considers that there is only one way that things can be.

Most children struggle to be who their narcissistic mother wants them to be, and she might start to resent them and become hostile toward them. She will punish the children in all kinds of ways, and use emotional threats; for example, she can threaten to leave them. The narcissistic mother will also not tolerate individuality or independence in their children.

A female covert narcissist is unable to form a genuine emotional connection with her children, and their relationship with her might be cold or distant. As they get older, the girls might be slammed for not meeting her expectations. The mother might even see the daughter as a competitor who takes the father's attention away from her.

How the Covert Narcissist Manipulates and Abuses Her Children

It can be difficult to recognize the abuse of a covert narcissist's children, as they often hide abuse and frame it as love.

When the narcissist acts in an abusive way toward her children, her past experiences of her own traumatic childhood shouldn't be used to excuse her current awful behavior. Adult children can also fall into the guilt trap of feeling sorry for their abusive mother as she experienced childhood trauma herself.

A covert narcissist may rely heavily on the assumption that all parents want the best for their children, and use this idea to disguise their unacceptable behavior. They will hold on to the persona of being "loving" parents. The truth is that the narcissistic mother lives in her own version of reality, which she maintains through lying.

The covert narcissistic mother may use microaggression to control her children, rather than openly hostile attacks. For example, she might criticize her children's appearance and abilities by using backhanded comments on their appearance, abilities, talents, or intelligence. A mother might tell her daughter she would be even prettier if she lost weight, or she has a pretty face, but she should probably consider plastic surgery on her nose one day when she can afford it.

The Victim

The covert narcissistic mother might also play the role of the innocent, sacrificing victim. She can avoid blame while getting sympathy from others. She will use guilt-tripping and pity plays to get attention from her children and others. It will become increasingly exhausting to listen to her negative stories of resentment, frustration, and anger.

It can be difficult for adult children to step away from having a relationship with her, as a result of feeling pity and guilt. They will feel guilty that they can't fix their mother's life and spare her some of the stress she is always experiencing. However, nothing can ever be good enough for her, as she needs to maintain her persona of victimhood.

The covert narcissistic mother likes to present herself as a devoted, caring, and self-sacrificing person. She can be adept at manipulating some family members, such as her preferred golden child. The children may also experience cognitive dissonance in this situation, as there is a definite gap between what they're told about this parent and how she behaves behind closed doors.

Some covert narcissistic mothers feel burdened by motherhood and neglect their children. When the children then want attention, they will criticize them for being needy. These mothers are needy themselves and can't also deal with their children's needs.

Narcissistic mothers may also use their children as part of triangulation within their marriage. Narcissists often struggle to be intimate with their partners and will bring a third party into the relationship because she is emotionally needy. This could be work, an addiction, or a lover, but often, the children are used in this way. She could use her children as confidants or companions. Children are ideal because she will find it easy to control them.

You also get families where both parents are narcissists. For example, you might get a malignant or overt narcissist that is very obviously abusive and has partnered with a covert narcissist who then plays her role as the good, selfless, and easygoing parent. She is also the long-suffering martyr who gives the children what caregiving they can get in this toxic environment.

The covert narcissist will pull out a heavier victim card when she senses that her children are pulling away from her, and she will become resentful if she senses that she is being discarded.

Her covert narcissistic behavior patterns can become significantly worse when she is experiencing a lot of stress in her life or if she has faced serious disappointment. This has confirmed her victimhood, which enrages her even more.

Covert narcissistic women will often have a quiet rage that floats just below the surface, that can erupt at any moment.

Plausible Deniability

The covert narcissistic mother will usually operate within plausible deniability. This means she will use indirect forms of manipulation and abuse, such as gaslighting, minimizing, triangulation, and redirection. If she is accused in the aftermath of her behavior, she will just deny it.

Plausible deniability can manifest in her behavior in the following ways:

- Plausible deniability can include behavior like gaslighting where they make their victims doubt their own perceptions of reality. They make it seem like the victim is overreacting, and they can deny their harmful behavior.
- Playing the victim is also part of plausible deniability, as they portray themselves as the ones who have been harmed to put themselves in a sympathetic light. It then becomes extremely difficult for others to hold them accountable.
- Indirect aggression or passive-aggressive behavior also allows them to distance themselves from events and they can claim they weren't responsible for the harm caused.

Unfortunately, children will continue to believe that their covertly abusive parent loves them, even if she displays cruel behavior toward them. They could even blame themselves if the relationship ultimately fails.

Uncovering patterns of narcissistic abuse when you look back as an adult can hurt like getting a hard blow to the stomach. It could take years to figure out the truth, but children will finally realize that they actually don't need this parent in their life and that they've actually always survived without their love.

Codependency

Children of covert narcissistic parents also run a high risk of becoming involved in a codependent relationship with a narcissist, as this partner replaces the mother since this is the type of behavior that they're used to.

Narcissistic mothers create codependent behavior in their children, as a result of their selfish, controlling behavior. While mature parents sacrifice their needs for the sake of their children, narcissists always put their needs ahead of those of their own children.

The children of these mothers then tend to become codependent, as they have to shift their needs and feelings aside to deal with those of their parents.

Narcissistic mothers will only really be involved with their children's activities and accomplishments if it reflects well on them, or if it was somehow their idea. Some of them start to live through their children and insist their children think, behave, and whatever else according to their wishes. There are those who will even make their children's life choices in adulthood if allowed to do so. They'll choose their children's careers, houses, cars, and even spouses.

Parentification

The female covert narcissist could also engage in the parentification of their children. They can expect their children to take on adult responsibilities such as taking care of their needs and providing emotional support.

Parentification can involve emotional caretaking where the child is expected to provide validation, attention, and emotional support to the mother. The narcissistic mother may treat the child like her confidant and share personal information like grievances and complaints with the child that is inappropriate for their age.

This could lead to the narcissistic mother blurring the boundaries with the child, treating them as an extension of herself, and establishing an enmeshed relationship. The child then ends up feeling overly responsible for the covert narcissistic mother's well-being.

As part of parentification, the child might also be burdened with household responsibilities that aren't appropriate for their age; for example, taking care of younger siblings or having to deal with financial matters.

Parentification can have a negative effect on the emotional growth of the child. The child could become anxious, feel inadequate, and build resentment.

The narcissistic mother may at times appear caring, but their behavior can quickly flip a switch and become controlling, and even shaming. Their love is conditional and their children will always be trying to please them and win their love.

It's easy for the covert narcissistic mother to manipulate her children by belittling, threatening, and guilt-tripping them. They'll shame and criticize their children, and call them names. They can ignore or criticize their children's normal feelings and needs. They will call a child sensitive and weak for expressing normal feelings. Their relationship with their children can become especially problematic when the children are teenagers and develop ideas of their own, which may not agree with their parents' ideas.

They will withdraw love to punish their children, making them insecure and teaching them that love is conditional. This abuse can be as damaging as physical and sexual abuse.

Effects in Adulthood

In adulthood, children of narcissistic mothers can struggle with anger and depression. They can feel abandoned and insecure and they don't know how to fulfill their own needs and set boundaries. They may feel like they don't exist as far as their parents are concerned, as their parents were never able to form an emotional connection with them.

Children of narcissistic mothers will continue to suffer until they accept their parent's limitations and start to make an effort to love themselves. Otherwise, it can be a lifelong journey of misery during which they relive the emotional suffering of their childhood. The unaware child of the narcissist will keep looking for validation in relationships with inappropriate partners such as addicts and narcissists.

The recovery of children of a covert narcissistic mother involves overcoming the codependency and shame they developed in their childhood.

Children of covert narcissistic mothers can grow up to be insecure and codependent. Their self-esteem and self-worth have always been undermined through verbal abuse, and they, therefore, struggle to develop an individual identity. They're used to accommodating their mothers' needs by suppressing their own needs and feelings. When they go on to have adult relationships, they still struggle to express feelings and needs. They could become people pleasers.

If the father didn't stand up to the covert narcissistic wife to protect the children from his wife's control, he didn't set an example for setting boundaries. This could cause the children to one day struggle to set boundaries in their adult relationships.

They need to learn to say "no" and to stand up for themselves. The fact is their narcissistic mother probably never allowed them to say no, and they could never do anything without being criticized.

Adult children of narcissistic mothers often have trouble connecting with who they really are. They are there to satisfy her needs, for example, so that she doesn't feel alone. The child's specific needs aren't noticed.

The child ends up not knowing who they really are, and might struggle to develop a sense of self in adulthood.

Adult children can also struggle with attachment and social relationships. They don't have healthy role models for emotional relationships as children, which means they may struggle with relationships and their social life when they're older.

These children may also face intimacy issues in their relationships. They were never safe to express their feelings and needs to their mother, and they may feel unsafe to do so in adult relationships. Children who have been manipulated and emotionally abandoned may fear being judged and abandoned by their partners.

Children who had an enmeshed relationship with their narcissistic mother may also fear that they will be controlled by their intimate partner. They could try to avoid intimacy, which means their partners will make more demands of them which will make the adult child of the narcissistic mother just more defensive and apprehensive.

Some adult children of narcissistic mothers may also struggle with narcissistic traits. They may have learned self-centered and manipulative behavior from their mother, and then replicate this behavior in their adult lives.

The emotional wounds of growing up with a narcissistic mother may also cause people to display narcissistic behavior in adulthood. The narcissistic traits can compensate for their insecurities.

It's important to recognize narcissistic traits and their underlying causes for the sake of personal growth and developing healthier relationships.

Coparenting With a Narcissist

Coparenting with a narcissist can be a nightmare, and is at best difficult. Narcissists can cause all kinds of problems in a coparenting arrangement. They're inflexible and struggle to stick to agreements. They'll use manipulation and try to put the children between the two of you when there is a disagreement.

Sometimes, you may need to opt for parallel parenting instead of coparenting. A parenting plan will then be set up that will minimize contact between the parents while allowing both to spend time with their children. The custody plan should be drawn up by legal professionals.

You need to prepare for an uphill battle if you share children with a narcissist, as they will likely try to turn the kids against you, or they will try to ruin your personal life.

Divorce is upsetting the covert narcissistic woman because it means a loss of control over their former partner. Even after they are divorced, they will create conflict with their former partner and blame any custody snags on the non-narcissistic parent. They will call and text you, and try to insert themselves in your personal life.

They may accuse you of things such as being a drug addict, or stalking and abusing them.

Parallel Parenting

Parallel parenting is a good option as it will allow you to have a legal agreement with strong boundaries and legal paperwork.

The best way you can prevent challenges while parallel parenting with your ex is to limit contact and communicate only in writing, where possible. If you communicate via email and text messaging, you can keep a record of what is said and you can keep evidence of harassment.

When the custody documents are set up, you need to be as specific as possible. Create explicit schedules for holidays, state that your privacy should be protected, and state that you would prefer to have limited contact with your ex. Every detail should be included in this agreement, for example, how many times a day phone calls will be allowed, and so on.

If your ex doesn't want to agree to a parallel parenting agreement, you'll have to leave the work to your lawyer. It's also a good idea to invest in a home security system that can record interactions with your ex if they ever come onto your property.

You'll never be able to protect your children entirely from the toxic influence of their narcissistic parent, but a parenting plan with strong guidelines and boundaries can protect them from parental fights.

A mediator that is appointed by the court can also help facilitate communication between parents. They can help resolve issues that you and your ex bring to court.

Guidelines for Parenting With the Narcissist

You need to keep certain things in mind when you parent with a narcissist:

- Think of your child and try to avoid getting caught up in your narcissistic ex's drama. Also, help your child recognize and work through their feelings. If they can verbalize what they're feeling, it will be easier for them to work through it.
- Don't speak ill of your narcissistic ex in front of your children. Keep complaints to yourself, as ranting in front of the kids will just put more pressure on them.

- Avoid emotional arguments with your ex and keep communication as neutral as possible. If you can work together regarding practical issues, it will make things easier for everyone.
- Make sure you have realistic expectations and expect that you will face challenges—then you will at least be prepared when issues do come your way.

Coparenting Story

Josh was a caring and devoted father of two children, Ben and Alice. He always had problems with his wife, Samantha, and he became aware that she was a female covert narcissist. After their relationship fell apart further, they decided to get divorced.

Josh became aware that it wasn't going to be easy to coparent with a covert narcissist.

He was hoping that they could put their differences aside for the sake of the children to make sure they got the best lives possible with both their parents, but Josh noticed that Samantha's manipulative and abusive behavior was getting worse. She undermined his authority and belittled his parenting decisions. She was also constantly looking for validation and attention.

Samantha started to play a game of control and used their children as pawns. She canceled plans at the last minute without warning Josh and badmouthed him to the children.

Josh found the experience emotionally draining and was worried that he couldn't give his best for the kids. Fortunately, he managed to find a therapist that treated personality disorders, who could help him understand the challenges of coparenting with a covert narcissist and how to deal with this difficult situation successfully.

Josh implemented boundaries and worked on establishing clear communication channels with Samantha. He used a shared parenting app to document discussions and important decisions. He knew there would be less possibility of manipulation taking place if he kept a record of their agreements and deviations from them.

The app also created a neutral environment in which to communicate and they didn't have to communicate face-to-face, which means there were fewer opportunities for disagreements and fighting.

However, Samantha continued to resist Josh's attempts to create a successful coparenting environment, and she accused him of being controlling.

A friend finally suggested that a mediator could possibly help them solve their coparenting issues. After the intervention of the mediator and many discussions later, Josh and Samantha finally managed to reach an agreement. They created a visitation schedule that was fair to all parties, developed consistent rules and strategies, and both committed to communicating in an open and respectful way.

The children also started to notice the positive changes. Their relationships with their parents improved and there was less conflict between their parents.

Activity: Template for Parenting Plan

A strict parenting plan can help you coparent with a narcissist and will be to the benefit of the child. You can use the following template to compile a plan. Each parent's role and responsibilities need to be clearly defined.

Pickup and drop-off locations	Pickups and drop-offs must take place in neutral and public locations, like the school, daycare, or community center. This will minimize contact between the parents.
Shared access to information	Both parents must have access to information about the child's education, healthcare, and extracurricular activities.
Guidelines for communication	Direct contact between the parents should be minimized, so as to reduce conflict and potential opportunities for manipulation. Use communication methods that can leave a documented trail, such as email or coparenting apps. Communication should be brief and focus on the necessities of the child.
Separate parenting time	Each parent should have enough uninterrupted time with the child.
Boundaries and self-care	Each parent needs to engage in self-care and in activities that will reduce their stress levels. If you're emotionally healthy, you'll be better equipped to coparent with a narcissist.
Consistency and stability for the child	The child should have a consistent and stable routine across both households. This can include similar rules and discipline strategies, which will make the child feel more secure.
Documented trail	Make sure that you keep a documented trail of all decisions that were made and challenges that were discussed.

Key Takeaways

- Children with narcissistic parents often struggle with self-esteem, as they have to shape themselves into who their parents want them to be.
- Narcissists often see their children as extensions of themselves and lose interest in them when they become adults.

- They regard the child's growing independence as a threat to their false persona.
- Children of narcissists can grow up to have insecure, codependent personalities. They can remember their childhoods as being uncomfortable and they suffered from anxiety while growing up.
- Children may struggle to see the behavior they suffered as abuse, especially if there was no physical abuse involved.
- A narcissist will always put herself first, even to the detriment of her own children.
- A female covert narcissist can't form a genuine emotional connection with her children. The relationship might be distant or cold.
- A covert narcissist might hide her unacceptable behavior and present herself as a loving parent.
- The "suffering victim" is a popular persona for the covert female narcissist.
- It's difficult for adult children to step away from having a relationship with the covert female narcissist, as they feel guilt and pity that they can't fix her life and save her from the stress she is experiencing. However, someone like this needs to maintain her status of victimhood.
- The narcissist's covert behavior patterns will become significantly worse in her life when she is experiencing stress. When her victimhood is "confirmed," she will be even angrier.
- Children of narcissists run a high risk of becoming involved in codependent relationships.
- Covert narcissistic women also tend to engage in the parentification of their young children. They expect

the children to provide emotional support to them and take on adult responsibilities.

- The narcissistic mother treats the child like her confidant and shares personal information with them.
- Children in an enmeshed relationship with a mother like this end up feeling overly responsible for her well-being.
- The covert narcissistic mother can appear loving at times, but her behavior can quickly change to controlling.
- Children can face problems in their future adult relationships.
- Coparenting with a narcissist can be a nightmare and it's best to have a legal agreement in place.
- Your ex can try to turn the children against you.
- You need to have a parallel parenting agreement with your narcissistic ex.

Conclusion

I hope that this book has opened your eyes to the behavior of other people around you, especially those with whom you want to have a meaningful relationship such as a romantic partnership. It is in your best interest not to form long-term relationships with toxic people.

NPD is a serious mental health disorder, which makes it extremely difficult to have meaningful relationships with others. There are also individuals who display narcissistic traits but they don't have NPD. The personality disorder can only be diagnosed by a qualified mental health practitioner.

Although this book focused on covert narcissism, there are different variants of this condition. Overt, covert, and malignant narcissism are the three most common forms.

Overt narcissism is the most recognizable form with individuals displaying an inflated sense of self-importance and grandiosity. These can be loud and attention-seeking people.

Conclusion

Covert narcissism is more subtle and narcissistic traits can even be hidden. These types of narcissists can play a victim role and then control others in subtle ways.

Malignant narcissists can also display antisocial and sadistic behavior. These types of narcissists can be dangerous, as they show no remorse for their often malicious and vindictive behavior.

The covert female narcissist wants you to know what her needs are without her having to tell you what they are. She also expects you to be attentive to her needs at all times.

The origin of narcissism can often be traced back to childhood trauma. While you shouldn't feel sorry for the narcissist, it's important to understand her behavior.

You can protect yourself from narcissists to an extent by setting boundaries. Setting boundaries threatens the narcissist's need to be in control. They will try to find loopholes in your boundaries and try to get past them.

If you do online dating, it's especially important to be wary of narcissists, as this type of dating gives them the perfect opportunity to present fake images of themselves to their potential targets.

There is a lot that can be said about being in a relationship with a female covert narcissist, but unfortunately nothing positive.

It's only after you've fallen for their fake persona that you'll get to know the real person who is prone to mood swings and narcissistic rage. They hold grudges, can become irrationally angry about small things, and suffer from explosive outbursts.

Conclusion

They only care about their own feelings and often ruminate about how others have done them wrong.

Nevertheless, it can be hard to end a relationship with a narcissist, as a result of trauma bonding. A trauma bond happens when you get attached to your abuser as a way of coping with your trauma. This is then reinforced through a cycle of abuse and reconciliation.

When you end your relationship with a narcissist, they can try to pull you back in by promising you that they will change. This will never happen and you'll just find yourself back in the same abusive situation.

Ultimately, the best thing to do for your mental and physical health is to end your relationship with the female covert narcissist, and then try to find yourself again through a well-managed healing process.

You'll feel a lot of anger, but it's necessary to experience and work through all your emotions before you move on. During the healing period, it's essential to focus on yourself and what you want from life.

A good therapist can help you develop your coping skills and you'll emerge as a more resilient person. Therapy can also prepare you to form healthier relationships in the future.

After ending an abusive relationship, you need to find a new purpose and meaning in your life. Sharing your experience with others who have experienced narcissistic abuse can help your healing process. By speaking out and raising awareness, you can help end the stigma around men who suffered emotional abuse.

Conclusion

I trust that this book has helped you feel less alone with your experience, and has given you a better understanding of the complex condition of covert female narcissism. If you need help in the future, I want to encourage you to refer back to the pages in the book.

Remember to be kind to yourself on your recovery journey and keep working toward a healthier and more meaningful future. After all, no one can love you as you can.

Leave A Review

If "Unmasking The Covert Female Narcissist" resonated with you, enlightened you, or offered solace during a challenging time, I'd love to hear from you. Reviews are more than just feedback; they are powerful testimonials that can help others seeking understanding or guidance on this intricate subject. By taking a few moments to share your thoughts, you not only validate the experiences and insights shared in the book but also assist potential readers in deciding if this is the resource they've been searching for. Every voice counts, and your unique perspective could be the beacon of hope for someone navigating the complexities of covert narcissism. Please consider leaving a review and becoming an integral part of this book's journey. Your words have the power to inspire and heal. Thank you for your support.

Glossary

- **Breadcrumbing:** A narcissist who wants to keep her options open can use this technique. They also use it when they're not ready for a relationship, but they want attention or affection. They will send suggestive messages without the intent of pursuing a relationship. They may even make future plans or promises, but they'll never follow through on anything. It is all a game for them. They lead the other person on to get control over them. Breadcrumbing can also be used as part of a narcissistic abuse campaign, to gain control over their partner.
- **Cognitive behavioral therapy (CBT):** This type of therapy focuses on the relationship between someone's thoughts, behavior, and feelings. CBT helps people identify their negative feelings and beliefs and develop a more balanced way of thinking.
- **Cognitive dissonance:** This is the tension between two or more conflicting beliefs, attitudes, or values

that a person might hold. They could feel guilt or shame when their actions and beliefs are in conflict with each other. For example, they know using drugs is bad for their health, but they continue using them. This can cause guilt or shame as their actions contradict each other. Cognitive dissonance can play a significant role in the behavior of narcissists. Their beliefs about their own superiority may conflict with reality. When the narcissist is confronted with reality, they can resort to behavior that reduces their discomfort, such as blaming others or distorting the truth to fit their false narrative. For example, if they're confronted at work by their manager for poor performance, they may launch a personal attack in retaliation.

- **Covert narcissist:** Covert narcissists are self-centered and self-absorbed in more subtle ways. They're usually more introverted and could appear modest and self-deprecating. However, this type of narcissist still has a sense of superiority and entitlement. They use their apparent sensitivity to manipulate everyone around them. Covert narcissists are usually skilled at hiding their true nature.

- **DARVO:** *DARVO* stands for "deny, attack, reverse victim, and offender." It's a tactic also used by narcissists to avoid taking responsibility and to shift the blame for something or to deflect criticism onto others. The narcissist can use this manipulative technique to stay in control of a situation (Freyd, 1997).

- **Flying monkeys:** Flying monkeys are enablers or supporters of the narcissist's abusive behavior. The flying monkeys could be friends, coworkers, family members, or sometimes even strangers who have been convinced by the narcissist's manipulation tactics. They do the narcissist's bidding by spreading rumors, acting as cyberbullies, or even directly attacking the narcissist's target. They usually think they're doing the right thing and might not realize they've been targeted by a narcissist.

- **Enmeshed relationship:** The narcissistic mother's manipulative behavior will blur boundaries and undermine the well-being of her children. There is a lack of healthy boundaries in this relationship, as well as emotional manipulation and a sense of emotional dependency can be created.

- **Future faking:** The narcissist makes promises and commitments for the future that they don't intend to keep. They could do this to suck a partner back into a toxic relationship, but they never follow through on the promises. It creates false hopes and expectations which can only lead to great disappointment for the narcissist's partner. It's important to be able to recognize this pattern to avoid being drawn in by it again.

- **Gaslighting:** Gaslighting occurs when someone is manipulated into doubting their version of reality and even their sanity. Narcissists may deny that something happened or tell their victims that they're imagining things. This is an insidious form of abuse as it usually happens so gradually that the victim might not realize what is happening.

- **Grey rock:** You can use this technique to minimize the attention you give a narcissist. It involves making yourself emotionally as uninteresting and unresponsive as you possibly can. Don't become involved in actions or conversations that give the other person something to use against you.

- **Hoover:** This refers to the technique the narcissist uses to try and suck a former partner back in a relationship and try and regain control over them. This can include constantly contacting the person, sending them gifts, or unexpectedly showing up at their home or workplace.

- **Hoover by proxy:** The narcissist will enlist a third party such as a friend or family member, to contact the person they're trying to control and manipulate. This could involve passing along messages and gifts. This could work to the advantage of the narcissist if their target feels pressured to respond to the third party, most likely if they have some kind of relationship with them.

- **Intermittent reinforcement:** The narcissist uses intermittent reinforcement to create unpredictability in a relationship, for example by giving their target attention and praising them, and then withdrawing it abruptly.

- **Lack of boundaries:** The narcissist may feel she is entitled to your time and attention. They won't respect your boundaries by doing things such as invading your privacy and personal space. If you request them not to do something, they will likely ignore you, as they feel their needs and desires are more important than yours.

- **Love bombing:** The narcissist uses love bombing to quickly gain someone's affection. They usually shower their target with gifts, attention, and affection. This may be flattering at first but is a red flag for a potentially dysfunctional relationship.

- **Malignant narcissist:** This type of narcissist also exhibits sociopathic traits. They're extremely entitled and believe they are superior to everyone around them. They're incapable of feeling guilt and remorse and will abuse others to reach their goals. It's difficult to deal with them, and they can be charming and charismatic.

- **Narcissistic abuse:** People who have narcissistic personality disorder (NPD) or narcissistic traits tend to abuse the people they have in their lives. Narcissistic abuse can take many forms, such as gaslighting and emotional blackmail, and can involve intimidation and manipulation to control the victim.

- **Narcissistic fog:** The victim of the narcissist finds themselves in this state of confusion when they are overwhelmed by the manipulation they experience from their partner, via manipulation and gaslighting. As a result of the influence of the narcissist, they're struggling to make decisions or think clearly.

- **Narcissistic fuel/supply:** This is the emotional energy or attention the narcissist needs from others to keep up the belief in their self-importance and superiority. Admiration, flattery, jealousy, and even fear can be narcissistic fuel. Narcissists try to get this type of energy from their family, friends, romantic partners, and even coworkers. Narcissistic fuel is the key component of their sense of self-worth and they will become angry and upset if they feel they're not getting enough.

- **Narcissistic personality disorder (NPD):** This condition is characterized by a lack of empathy for others, an inflated sense of self, and a belief that one is superior to others. They may have an exaggerated belief in their abilities and talents. Narcissists have difficulty maintaining healthy relationships and they may struggle to cope with rejection and criticism. This condition can only be diagnosed by a mental health professional through a comprehensive assessment.

- **Narcissistic rage:** This is the narcissist's intense emotional reaction when their sense of superiority or entitlement is challenged in some way. This rage can take many different forms; for example, explosive outbursts of anger that might make it appear as if the narcissist has completely lost their mind, physical or verbal abuse such as belittling their partner, or a withdrawal of attention and affection. Although the narcissist may appear as if they have lost their mind during this outburst of temper, they are in control of their actions and need to be held responsible for their behavior. This explosive behavior is the way in which they have chosen to act.

- **No contact:** This refers to completely cutting off contact with the narcissist to prioritize your own physical and mental well-being. It can involve blocking their phone number and removing them from your social media accounts.

- **Overt narcissist:** An overt narcissist looks for attention and admiration in a very obvious and conspicuous way. They're usually loud and confident, lack empathy, and exploit others for their own gain. They will become angry and defensive if you challenge them.

- **Post-traumatic stress disorder (PTSD):** This mental health condition can develop in people who have experienced traumatic events. This can include assault, abuse, accidents, and natural disasters. The symptoms of PTSD are nightmares, flashbacks, or intrusive thoughts, as well as avoiding people or places that may trigger memories of the trauma. PTSD can make it difficult for someone to function in their daily life. You can suffer PTSD as a result of narcissistic abuse, as it causes psychological trauma. Victims of narcissistic abuse can also develop complex PTSD (C-PTSD) which is caused by repeated trauma.

- **Plausible deniability:** This concept can be connected to the narcissist's abusive and manipulative behavior. It refers to their ability to create circumstances or behavior that allow them not to take responsibility for their actions. It involves situations where they can claim innocence even when they have been involved or they know about the situation. Examples of plausible deniability behavior can include gaslighting, playing the victim, and indirect aggression.
- **Psychoanalytic therapy:** This therapy is based on exploring a person's unconscious thoughts, memories, and emotions that may be influencing the way they behave and their mental health. A psychoanalytic therapist can also use techniques such as dream analysis and free association.
- **Push-pull behavior:** This refers to a common type of behavior from the narcissist when they're intensely interested in you at one moment, and the next moment they become distant. This causes the people in their life to feel confused about the status of the relationship.

- **Rumination:** Rumination involves repetitive thinking about negative experiences and situations, as well as dwelling on past events or failures. This way of thinking can lead to stress, anxiety, and even depression. It also prevents people from finding solutions to their problems.
- **Smear campaign:** Narcissists use this tactic to damage the reputation or reputation of someone they either see as a threat or the person who has rejected their advances. This campaign involves spreading rumors, manipulating others to turn them against the target, and making false accusations.
- **Somatic narcissist:** Somatic narcissists focus on their physical appearance, and they're obsessed with their bodies, clothes, and how sexually attractive they are. They may boast about their sexual conquests. They use their physical attributes as a way to get attention and admiration.
- **Stonewalling:** Stonewalling is a tactic where one person withdraws from a conversation or shuts it down. It can involve silent treatment where the person refuses to engage in communication or conversation with someone else. Narcissists use stonewalling to maintain control of their relationships.
- **Trauma bond:** A trauma bond can occur when a victim becomes emotionally attached to a perpetrator as a way of coping with trauma. This bond is often reinforced through a cycle of abuse and reconciliation. The trauma bond can make it difficult for the victim to leave the relationship as they become dependent on the abuser for some form of validation.

- **Triangulation:** Triangulation involves bringing a third party into a disagreement to create instability and confusion. The narcissist can use a third party to undermine their target's credibility.

- **Vulnerable narcissist:** A vulnerable narcissist is someone who has a fragile self-esteem, and displays narcissistic tendencies. They want attention and empathy while presenting themselves as sensitive victims. They're usually only concerned with their own emotional needs and don't have empathy for others. The terms "vulnerable narcissist" and "covert narcissist" are often used interchangeably.

- **Word salad:** Word salad occurs when a person strings together words and phrases in a way that makes it difficult to understand their intended meaning or follow their train of thought. The narcissist uses word salad as a deliberate strategy to confuse others. Narcissists also use world salad to escape responsibility for their actions.

References

Adler, L. (2021, March 22). *7 devious traits of a covert female narcissist.* Toxic Ties. https://toxicties.com/covert-female-narcissist-traits/

Akin, E. (2022, November 24). *5 ways that narcissists isolate you.* Unfilteredd. https://unfilteredd.net/how-do-narcissists-isolate-you/

Arabi, S. (2017, August 21). *11 signs you're the victim of narcissistic abuse.* PsychCentral. https://psychcentral.com/blog/recovering-narcissist/2017/08/11-signs-youre-the-victim-of-narcissistic-abuse#3

Arabi, S. (2019, October 23). *Can you spot a narcissist online? 3 surprising behaviors which reveal predators in cyberspace.* PsychCentral. https://psychcentral.com/blog/recovering-narcissist/2019/10/can-you-spot-a-narcissist-online-3-surprising-behaviors-which-reveal-predators-in-cyberspace#1

Arabi, S. (2020 May 18). *Online dating is a hunting ground for narcissists and sociopaths: How to protect yourself in the modern dating age.* Thought Catalog. https://thoughtcatalog.com/shahida-arabi/2017/12/narcissists-rule-the-online-dating-world-how-to-protect-yourself-in-the-modern-dating-age/

Clarke, J. (2023, April 25). *How to recognize someone with covert narcissism.* Verywell Mind. https://www.verywellmind.com/understanding-the-covert-narcissist-4584587

Collier, L. (2016, November). *Growth after trauma.* American Psychological Association. https://www.apa.org/monitor/2016/11/growth-trauma

Corelli, C. (2023, February 6). *The 10 stages of healing after narcissistic abuse: What to expect and how to cope.* Carla Corelli. https://www.carlacorelli.com/narcissistic-abuse-recovery/the-10-stages-of-healing-after-narcissistic-abuse-what-to-expect-and-how-to-cope/

Cuncic, A. (2021, November 18). *Effects of narcissistic abuse.* Verywell Mind. https://www.verywellmind.com/effects-of-narcissistic-abuse-5208164

Dorwart, L. (2022, January 21). *Narcissistic personality disorder types.* Verywell Health. https://www.verywellhealth.com/narcissistic-personality-disorder-types-5213256

Estrada, J. (2023, February 18). *"I'm a psychologist, and this is why having*

References

narcissistic tendencies doesn't automatically make you a bad person." Well+Good. https://www.wellandgood.com/narcissism-vs-narcissistic-tendencies/

Firestone, L. (2013, April 29). *In a relationship with a narcissist? A guide to narcissistic relationships.* PsychAlive. https://www.psychalive.org/narcissistic-relationships/

Fjelstand, M. (2017, June 22). *8 things to expect when you break up with a narcissist (A relationship specialist explains).* Mindbodygreen. https://www.mindbodygreen.com/articles/what-to-expect-when-you-break-up-with-a-narcissist

Freyd, J. J. (1997). Violations of power, adaptive blindness and betrayal trauma theory. *Feminism & Psychology, 7*(1), 22–32. https://doi.org/10.1177/0959353597071004

Gaba, S. (2019, October 10). *The role a narcissistic mother can play in codependency.* Medium. https://medium.com/@SherryGaba/the-role-a-narcissistic-mother-can-play-in-codependency-7a30cf3b8a1c

Gillis. K. (n.d.). *9 narcissistic manipulation tactics & how to deal.* Choosing Therapy. https://www.choosingtherapy.com/narcissistic-manipulation-tactics/

Greenberg, E. (2019, March 19). *Do narcissists feel guilty about abusing loved ones?* Psychology Today. https://www.psychologytoday.com/za/blog/understanding-narcissism/202203/do-narcissists-feel-guilty-about-abusing-loved-ones

Hall, J, (2017, March 3). *Why you should not feel sorry for the narcissist.* HuffPost. https://www.huffpost.com/entry/why-you-should-not-feel-sorry-for-the-narcissist_b_58b7433ae4b0563cd36f646a

Heyl, J. C. (2022, June 23). *Finding a narcissistic abuse support group.* Verywell Mind. https://www.verywellmind.com/how-to-find-a-narcissistic-abuse-support-group-5271477

Heyl, J. C. (2022, December 14). *What is C-PTSD from narcissistic abuse?* Verywell Mind. https://www.verywellmind.com/c-ptsd-narcissistic-abuse-5225119

Kalt, M. (2022, May 6). *Does a covert narcissist actually struggle with setting boundaries?* ILLUMINATION. https://medium.com/illumination/does-a-covert-narcissist-actually-struggle-with-setting-boundaries-4857bb1823b4

Kaufman, S. B. (2020, April 20). *Post-traumatic growth: Finding meaning and creativity in adversity.* Scientific American. https://blogs.scientificamerican.com/beautiful-minds/post-traumatic-growth-finding-meaning-and-creativity-in-adversity/

Lancer, D. (2021, March 21). *Why narcissists and abusers won't let go and*

References

what you can do. Psychology Today. https://www.psychologytoday.-com/us/blog/toxic-relationships/202103/why-narcissists-and-abusers-wont-let-go-and-what-you-can-do

Lancer, J. D. (2022, February 4). *Having a narcissistic parent. What is codependency?* https://whatiscodependency.com/the-narcissistic-parent/

Lebow, H. (2018, December 11). *Narcissism vs. narcissistic personality: How to tell the difference.* Psych Central. https://psychcentral.com/disor-ders/narcissistic-personality-disorder/the-difference-between-narcissism-narcissistic-personality-disorder#traits-vs-personality-disorder

Love With Intelligence. (n.d.). *Why boundaries won't help with narcissists.* https://www.lovewithintelligence.com/boundary-setting-with-narcissists

McBride, K. (2018, February 19). *How narcissistic parenting can affect children.* Psychology Today. https://www.psychologytoday.-com/za/blog/the-legacy-of-distorted-love/201802/how-narcissistic-parenting-can-affect-children

Mind Tools Content Team. (2022). *SMART goals.* Mind Tools. https://www.-mindtools.com/a4wo118/smart-goals

Mishra, A. (2022, December 6). *Breaking up with a narcissist: 7 tips and what to expect.* Bonobology.com. https://www.bonobology.-com/breaking-up-with-narcissist/

Mitjana, L. R. (2022, September 23). *Narcissistic parenting and its effects on children.* Exploring Your Mind. https://exploringyourmind.-com/narcissistic-parenting-and-its-effects/

Mitra, P., & Fluyau, D. (2022, May 1). Narcissistic personality disorder. In *StatPearls [Internet].* StatPearls Publishing. https://www.ncbi.nlm.nih.gov/books/NBK556001/

Moore, A. (2020, April 27). *There are at least 8 types of narcissists — Which ones are dangerous?* Mindbodygreen. https://www.mindbody-green.com/articles/types-of-narcissists

Narcissistic Abuse Rehab. (2019). *The narcissist's childhood trauma (covert narcissism)* [Video]. YouTube. https://www.youtube.com/watch?v=BQn9JPE4wPg

Neo, P. (2018, February 5). *8 unexpected ways a narcissist isolates you.* Mindbodygreen. https://www.mindbodygreen.com/articles/8-ways-a-narcissist-isolates-you

Patricia. (2021, June 10). *What is the difference between an overt and a covert narcissist?* Inner Toxic Relief. https://innertoxicrelief.-com/difference-between-overt-and-covert-narcissist/

Rice, M. (2022, August 17). *Covert narcissism: Signs, traits, & how to handle it.* Talkspace. https://www.talkspace.com/mental-health/condi-tions/narcissistic-personality-disorder/types/covert-narcissism/

References

Robinson, L., & Segal, J. (2019, March 28). *Volunteering and its surprising benefits.* HelpGuide.org. https://www.helpguide.org/articles/healthy-living/volunteering-and-its-surprising-benefits.htm

Schneider, A. (2013, June 7). *Recovering from narcissistic abuse, part I: Blindsided.* GoodTherapy.org Therapy Blog. https://www.goodthera-py.org/blog/blindsided-recovering-narcissistic-abuse-relationship-0607134

Shafir, H. (2022, November 9) *Female narcissist: 15 common traits to look for.* Choosing Therapy. https://www.choosingtherapy.com/female-narcissist/

Shea, E. (2021, November 17). *The power of sharing your story.* Abuse Refuge Org. https://abuserefuge.org/the-power-of-sharing-your-story/

The Silent Wave. (2021, September 13). *8 early red flags you're dating a covert narcissist.* Medium. https://thesilentwave.medium.com/8-early-red-flags-youre-dating-a-covert-narcissist-efc1bc6b9640

Stillwaggon Swan, L. (2021, July 12). *What is resilience?* Psychology Today. https://www.psychologytoday.com/intl/blog/the-philosopher-is-in/202107/what-is-resilience

Telloian, C. (2021, September 15). *How many types of narcissism are there?* Psych Central. https://psychcentral.com/health/types-of-narcissism

The Mend Project. (2021, February 2). *Why sharing your story of abuse is one of the most powerful things you could ever do.* https://themendpro-ject.com/why-sharing-your-story-of-abuse-is-one-of-the-most-powerful-things-you-could-ever-do/

Tracy, N. (2020). *Emotional abuse of men: Men victims of emotional abuse too.* HealthyPlace. https://www.healthyplace.com/abuse/emotional-psychological-abuse/emotional-abuse-of-men-men-victims-of-emotional-abuse-too

Wade, D. (2020, July 27). *12 signs you might have narcissistic victim syndrome.* Healthline. https://www.healthline.com/health/narcissistic-victim-syndrome

Walder, C. (2022, May 16). *Understanding the children of a narcissist.* The Better You Institute. https://thebetteryouinstitute.-com/2022/05/16/children-of-a-narcissist/

Waters, S. (2022, April 13). *Healthy boundaries in relationships: A guide for building and keeping.* BetterUp. https://www.betterup.-com/blog/healthy-boundaries-in-relationships

Western Connecticut State University. (2018). *Benefits of community service.* https://www.wcsu.edu/community-engagement/benefits-of-volunteering/

Wilson, R. E. (2022, August 7). *Narcissists delight as pandemic boosts*

References

online dating. Psychology Today. https://www.psychologytoday.-com/za/blog/the-main-ingredient/202008/narcissists-delight-pandemic-boosts-online-dating

Zoë Ross Psychotherapy. (n.d.). *Narcissistic abuse therapy & counselling*. https://www.zoeross.com/narcissistic-abuse-therapy/

Made in United States
Troutdale, OR
12/07/2024

26068062R00089